African Drum Music
INCIDENCE ANALYSIS

Kongo Zabana

Published for
INTERNATIONAL CENTRE OF AFRICAN MUSIC AND DANCE

 **Afram Publications (Ghana) Limited**

Published for
International Centre of African Music and Dance

Published by
Afram Publications (Ghana) Ltd.
P.O. Box M. 18
Accra, Ghana

© **Kongo Zabana, 1997**

All rights reserved, No part of this publication may be reproduced, stored in a retrieval system, or transmitted in any form or by any means, electronic, mechanical, photocopying, recording or otherwise, without the prior written permission of Afram Publications (Ghana) Limited.

First Published: 1997

ISBN 9964-70-215-9

Printed by
Fredieko Ventures Ltd
P. O. Box 292
Darkuman- Accra
Tel: 231177

FOREWORD

When African musicians play in drum ensembles, one of them may play a rhythm pattern on a bell or some other instrument to establish a time line for the piece. The pattern played in this manner is fixed for the particular piece and a number of other pieces in the same general style. When the time line is sounded and repeated as a continuous cyclical pattern, each drummer begins his rhythm pattern at a specific point within it soon after it starts, or where preferred, at a point within the rhythm pattern of an other instrument to which his part is closely related. These points of entry which may be different for each instrument are also predetermined for each piece. Hence performing in a drum ensemble means not only knowing the role one's instrument is supposed to play in the totality but also the rhythm or rhythms assigned to it and precisely where they fit into the music, for in this style of drumming, every drum piece is a composition in the sense that it has its characteristic rhythms, internal relationships and performance practices that allow for spontaneous variations as well as the application of procedures for sustaining it in performance for as long as the situation demands.

Because of the different rhythm patterns assigned to the various drums, drum pieces conceived in this style present special problems for the listener owing to the complex texture that emerges from the different layers of rhythm. While one or two notes of each drum may stand out in a given cycle of events, others may overlap or interlock with notes played by other drums. That is why beginners are told, during performance, to concentrate on their own part after listening to the bell or some other instrument for their point of entry, for they could be easily distracted by the parts of the other drums. Dancers similarly have to learn not only how to listen but also what to listen for or respond to in drumming. Hence it is only frequent participation in drumming or exposure to it that enables the individual to get to know particular pieces and gradually over come some of these difficulties.

As opportunities for learning to understand and appreciate drumming in contemporary contexts through such experiences are no longer as frequent as they used to be, there is a need for recordings that will enable interested individuals to listen to the performance of particular drum pieces over and over again and absorb some of their essential characteristics. Analytical recordings which allow one to listen to each drum separately and in combination with another instrument can, to some extent, also help to clarify this complexity as they enable the listener to figure out the constituents of the patterns that are played. For the musically literate musician, the process of aural analysis can be greatly facilitated by transcriptions *in extenso* that provide a visual display of the basic score of the performance of a drum piece. He can study the parts of the ensemble a little more systematically or in some detail at his leisure, with particular reference to the compositional techniques of different pieces or performance practices and procedures as he notes the particular selection of rhythm patterns that make up each piece and how they all relate to one another. He could look at the particular rhythms that give definition or identity to the piece, those that support or complement other rhythms, those that contribute to the sonority complex or fullness of texture as well as variants and invariants and the manner in which changes in rhythmic progressions are effected by a master drummer.

In addition to deepening one's understanding and appreciation of drumming in the foregoing manner, the contemporary musician interested in creative performance or composition can use such scores in his own way. He could quote some of the materials or derive cells from patterns and subject them to various derivations. He could use the score of a drum piece in part or in whole as the rhythm section for the melodic parts of a composition in much the same way as such scores are used in traditional contexts.

Just as transcriptions of traditional songs provide source materials for music education, so may the scores of drum music be used in a similar manner -- as *aide memoire* for learners, as source for rhythmic exercises, as materials that may be set to nonsense syllables and performed as spoken drum texts as it is customary in traditional practice. It is with these and other uses in mind that the International Centre for African Music and Dance at the University of Ghana has embarked on this project aimed at making African drum music accessible to a wider public in the form of musical scores, audio and video recordings. Although one is dealing essentially with music cultivated and practiced by oral tradition, the value of transcriptions is not disputed by African musicians.

This series of scores of drum music has been prepared within the framework of this project. They are examples of drum music in Ghana computerized by Dr. Kongo Zabana, Senior Fellow at the International Centre for African Music and Dance, so that the basic scores emerging from this process might be accessible to musicians and educators, students, performers, composers as reference or source materials. They were generated in collaboration with the traditional master drummers of the Ghana Dance

Ensemble, all of whom are experts recruited from their ethnic communities. Students at the School of Performing Arts hear them from a distance everyday as they rehearse. Those in music and dance are generally required to learn to play a few of the pieces they play by rote and imitation with the help of their own traditional instructors. It seems, however, that the absence of a complete set of scores of the current repertoire of drum pieces retards their progress and also often prevents them from applying the analytical techniques they learn in other contexts to this body of materials. Other students elsewhere also go through the same process of learning some of this repertoire by rote and imitation without fully analyzing this experience. The immediate objective of this series of books of scores of drum music is, therefore, practical—to have in place a body of materials that can enrich local teaching programmes but which can also be shared by other interested musicians.

As the scores are intended as aids to analytical understanding and appreciation of drum music, they are written in notation familiar to potential users of the materials. Both the full score and the separate individual parts are presented in their basic form, that is, without the addition of accents and other performance symbols that may be idiosyncratic of the style of an individual performer. Rhythms that are framed within contrasting sonorities are written on either side of a single line or on two lines where appropriate.

To enable the vertical alignments of the different attack or "incidence" points to be readily seen, the transcriptions focus on these where appropriate and not always on the total duration of the sounds that emerge.

Similarly analytical commentary or discussion of the interrelations of drumming and dancing and associative meanings fall beyond the scope of the present project. Those interested in such problems will find the select bibliography very helpful. Our objective is simply to facilitate discovery of the cognitive foundations of African drum music.

Legon
August, 1997

J. H. KWABENA NKETIA
Director ICAMD

PREFACE

Sometimes it happens in a society that elder minds choose others to assume a happy paternal role for a collective action which should be better attributed to them, since they spend almost as much time as those they select, checking and orientating *their* perspectives as well as lending them a helping hand in the main mental and practical operations. Let me gratefully recognize that this happened to me with Professor J. H. Kwabena Nketia who is the real mastermind behind this *African Drum Music* series. Any eventual deficiencies should be blamed on my own technical experience.

This booklet is also the fruit of an incredible conjunction of efforts from more persons than I can mention by name.

I would like to acknowledge in particular the master drummers of the Ghana Dance Ensemble (Legon), Messrs. Ofori Adade and Solomon Amanquan-doh, Kwasi Nyantakyi, Rocky Atsu and John Osei whose full performance and mnemonics are reflected in these scores. What is to be emphasized is not only what they did - because they agreed to transmit their knowledge to us in private -, but also the way they did it, because it is not so common to seriously enjoy doing so, as they did.

I owe special thanks to Dr. N. Fiagbedzi, Senior Lecturer in the Music Department of the School of Performing Arts, for his help in transcribing *Ewe* mnemonics supplied by the master drummers mentioned earlier on.

I am also indebted to my friends Efo Kosi Adom and Maxwell Agyei Addo, for the time they spent to organize photographic sessions for the illustrations in this series.

To all the ICAMD's administrative staff and special persons involved in the completion of this booklet, I owe a big debt of gratitude.

Legon,
August, 1997

KONGO Zabana

CONTENTS

Performance practice and instruments	1
Full score	2
Note on Atsimevu	37
Vertical alignment	38
Gakogui and axatse	38
Gakogui and kagan	39
Gakogui and totodzi	40
Gakogui and kroboto	41
Gakogui and kidi	42
Gakogui and Atsimevu	44
Bibliography	58

PERFORMANCE PRACTICE AND INSTRUMENTS

The Agbekor dances are widely distributed among the Ewe of Ghana and variants are found even in Benin from where the Anlo Ewe speaking people migrated. Agbekor is essentially a soldiers' dance like the Asonko dance of the Twi people. To watch scenes which may have their actual origins in the battles that were fought as the Anlo trekked through hostile country in search of peace.

The slow Agbekor is processional in the original form and illustrates the trekking. It is marked at intervals with halts during which, short episodes are danced. Some epidodes reflect moments of relaxation when the warriors play games.

The Atsiagbekor is made up of modern inventions based on the older Agbekor. Atsia, like the Twi akyea means to show off and is the modern Anlo's version of what must have been a serious expression of prowess, suffering, and hardship by people who had to battle. In effect they are stylisations of Western arms drill blended with the traditional movements. The Dancers tend to show off with movements which display agility, physique and strength.

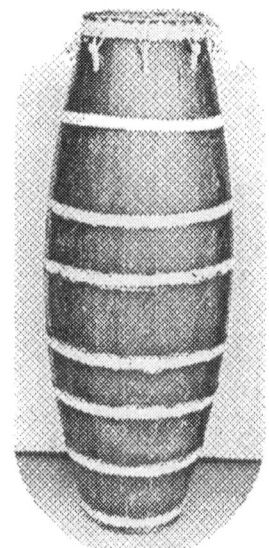

Atsimevu (main drum)

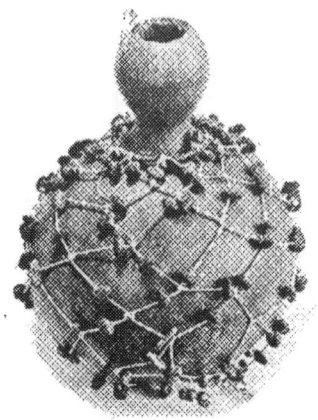

Axatse (rattle)

USUAL INSTRUMENTAL SET
Bell: Gakogui
Rattle: Axatse
Drums: Kagan, Totodzi, Kroboto, Kidi, Atsimevu

Slow Agbekor

Full score

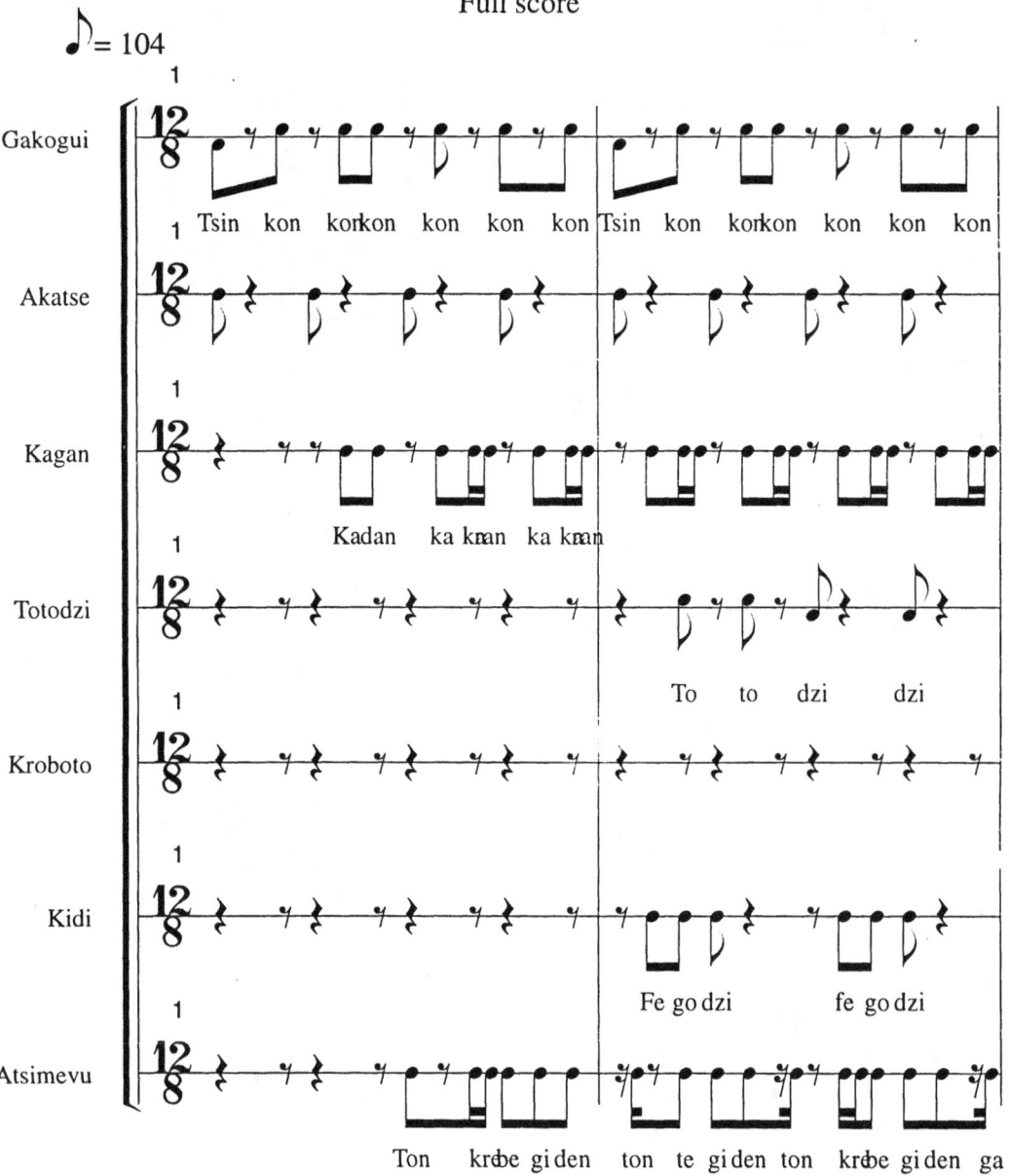

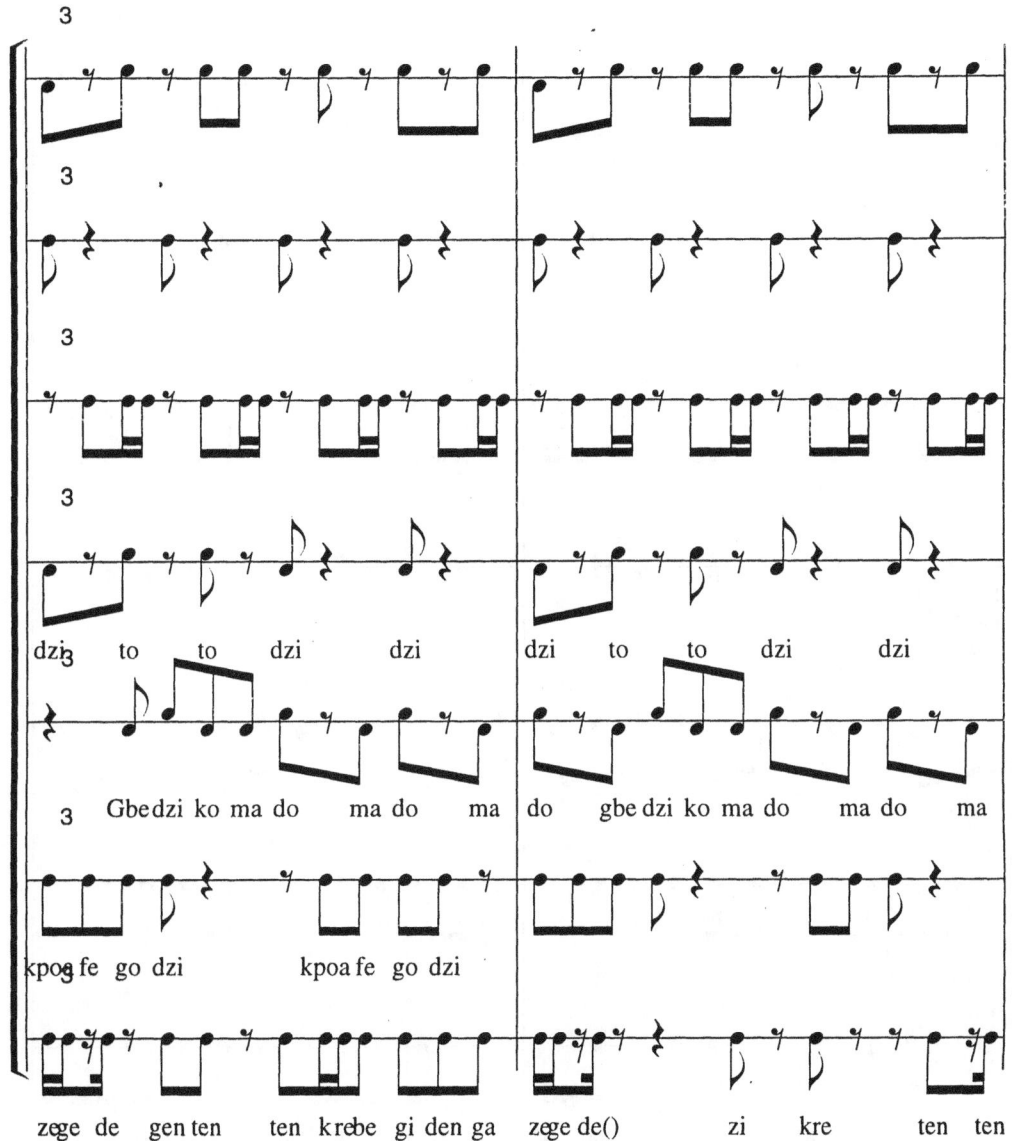

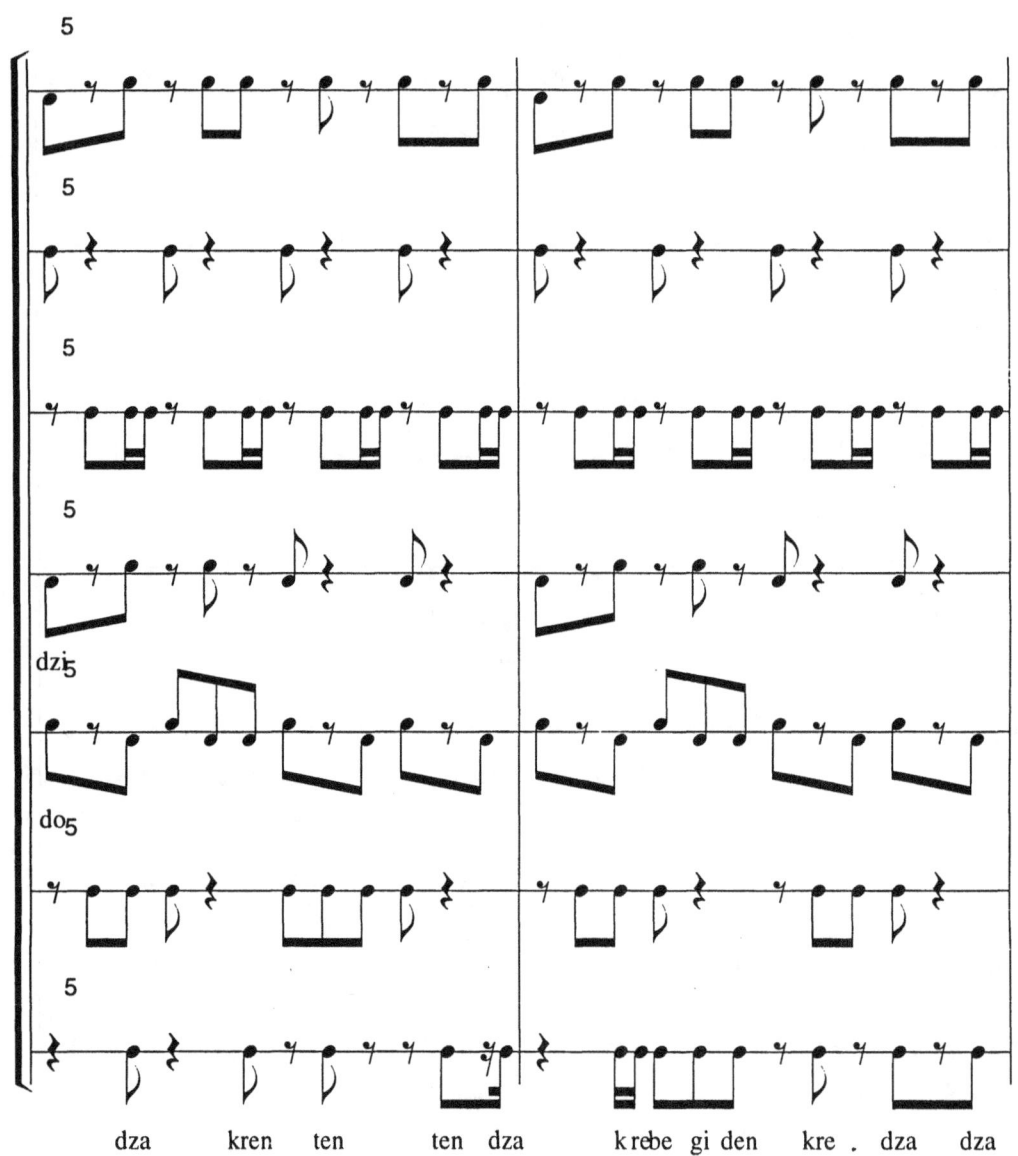

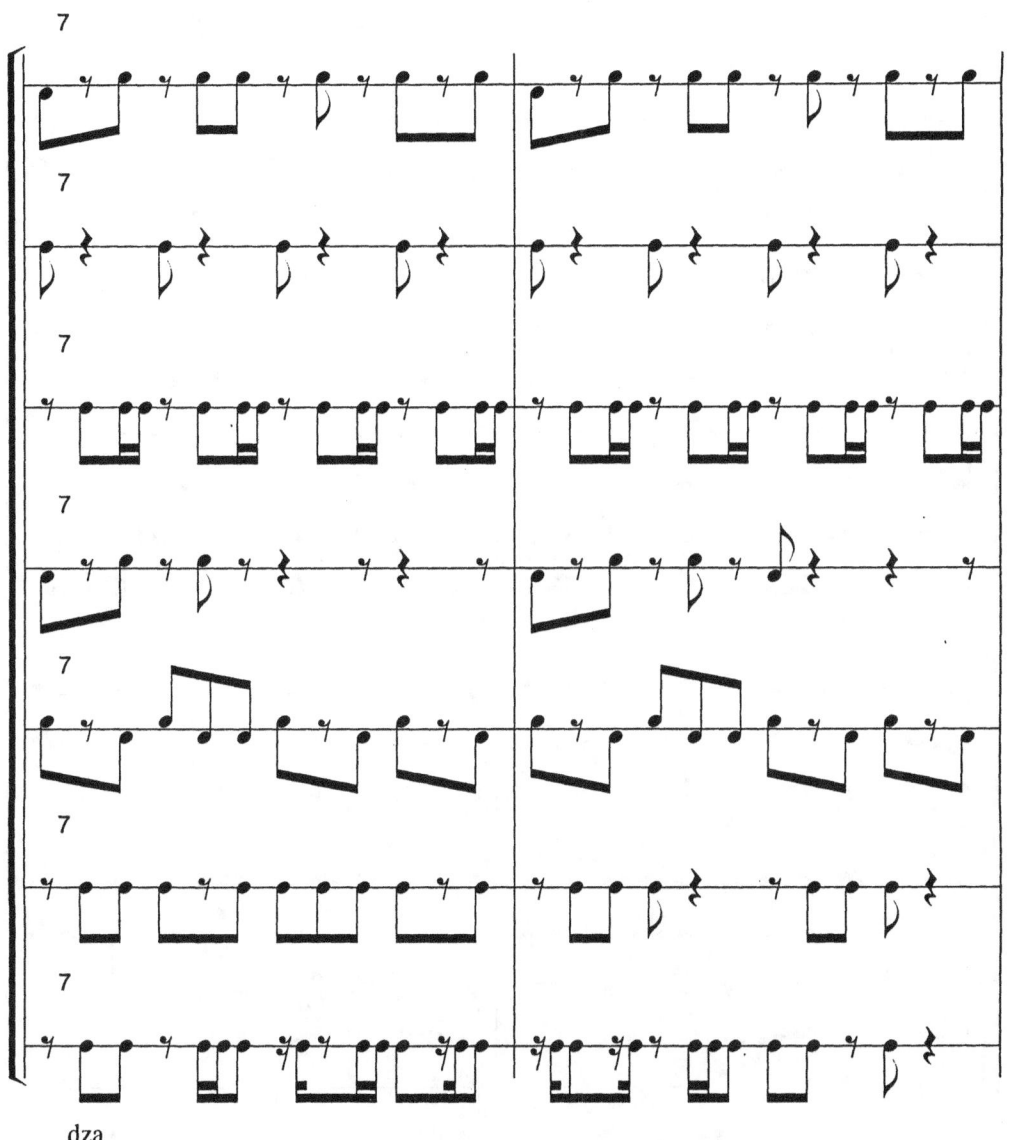

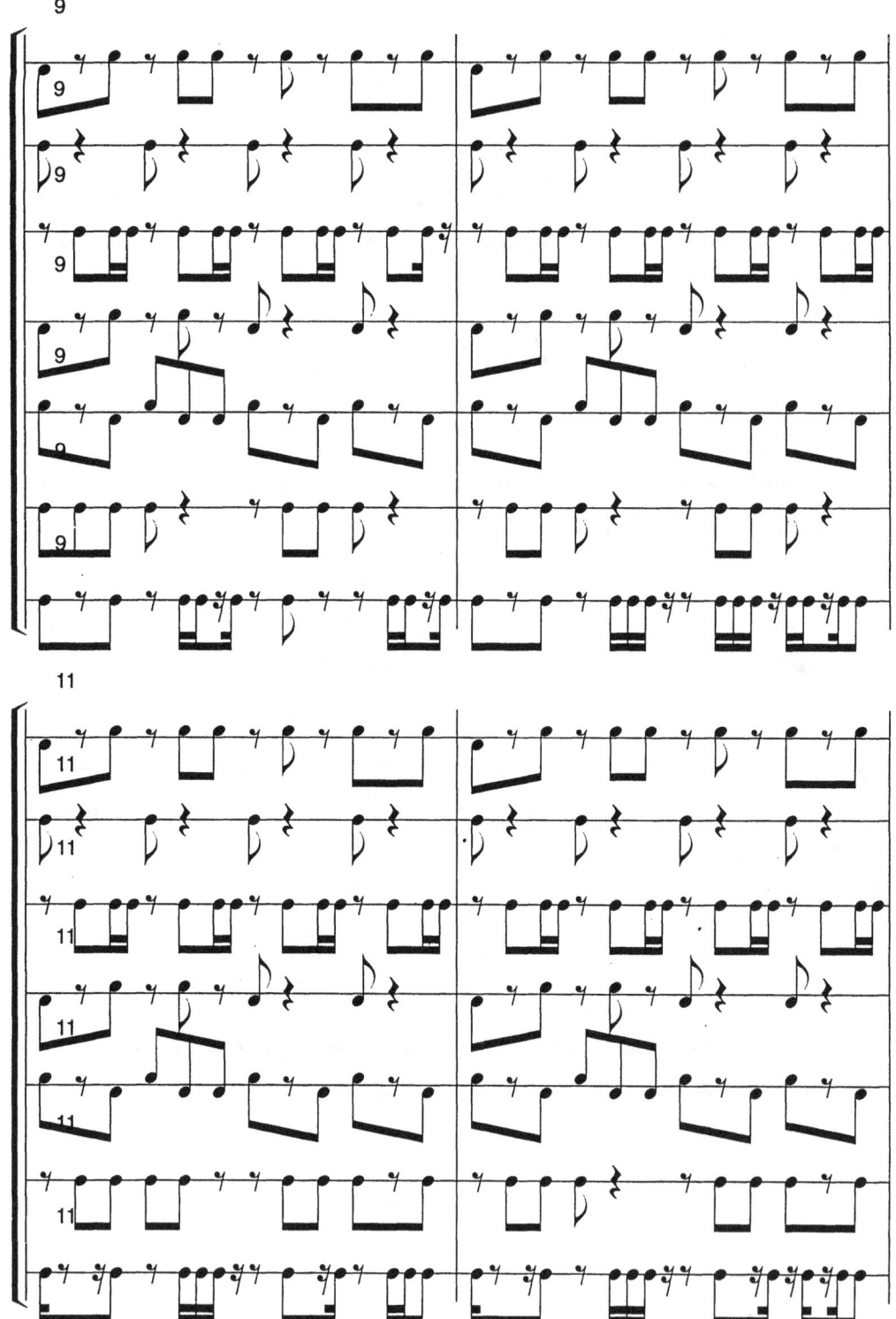

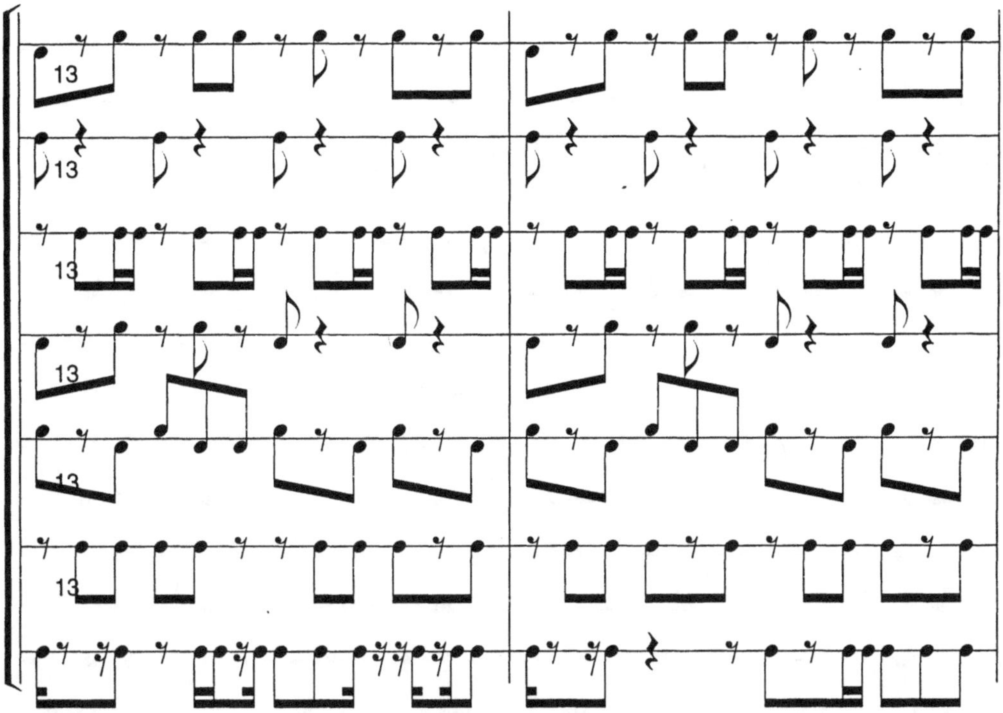

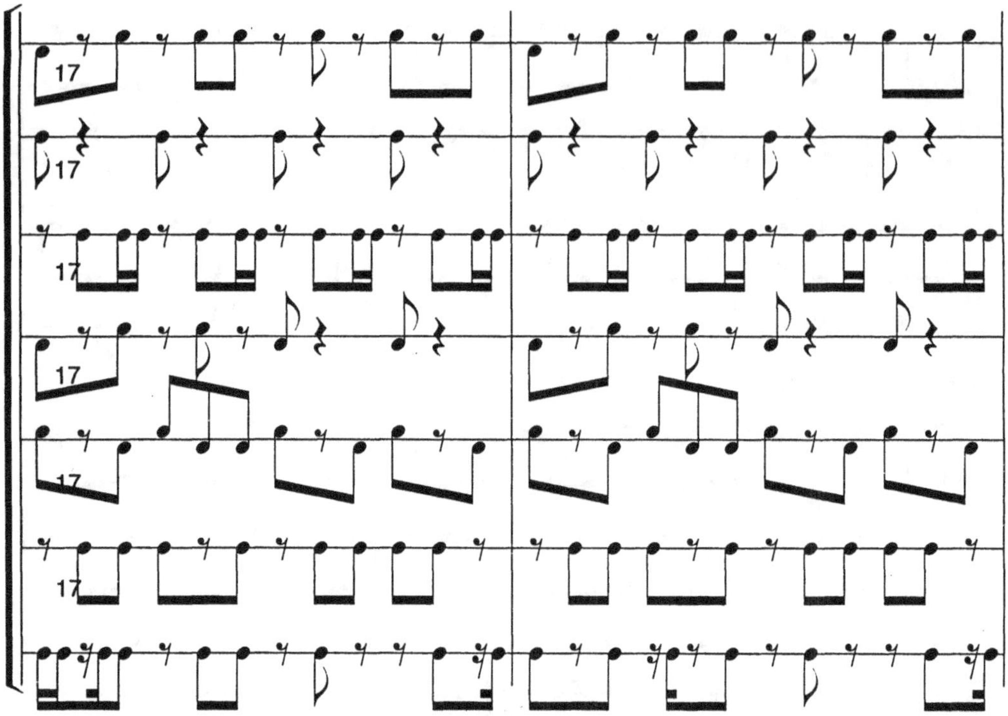

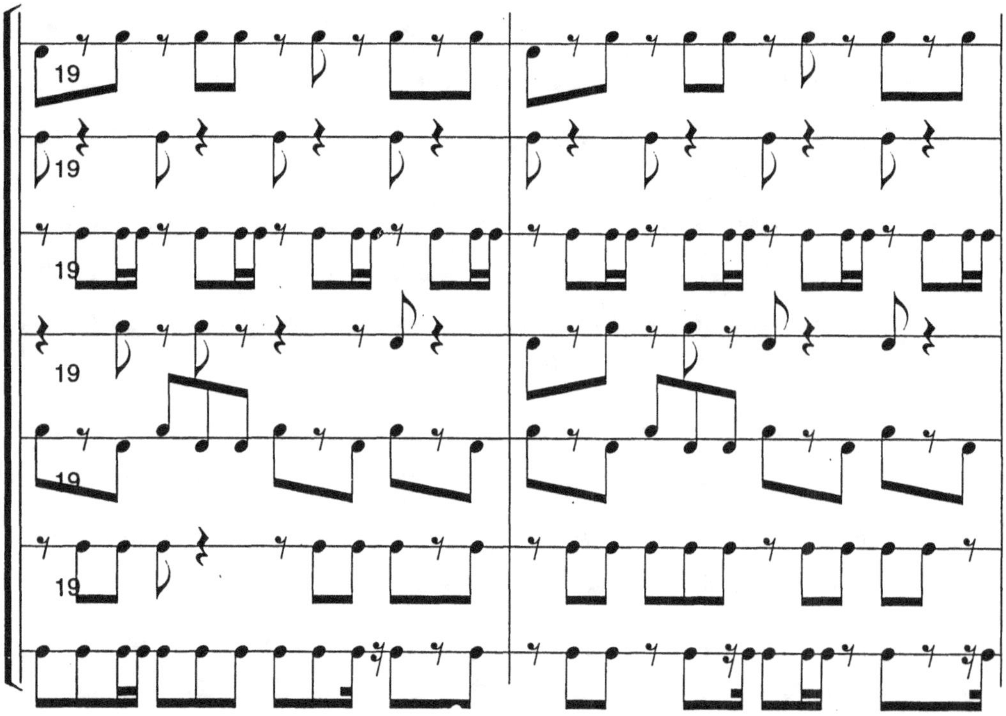

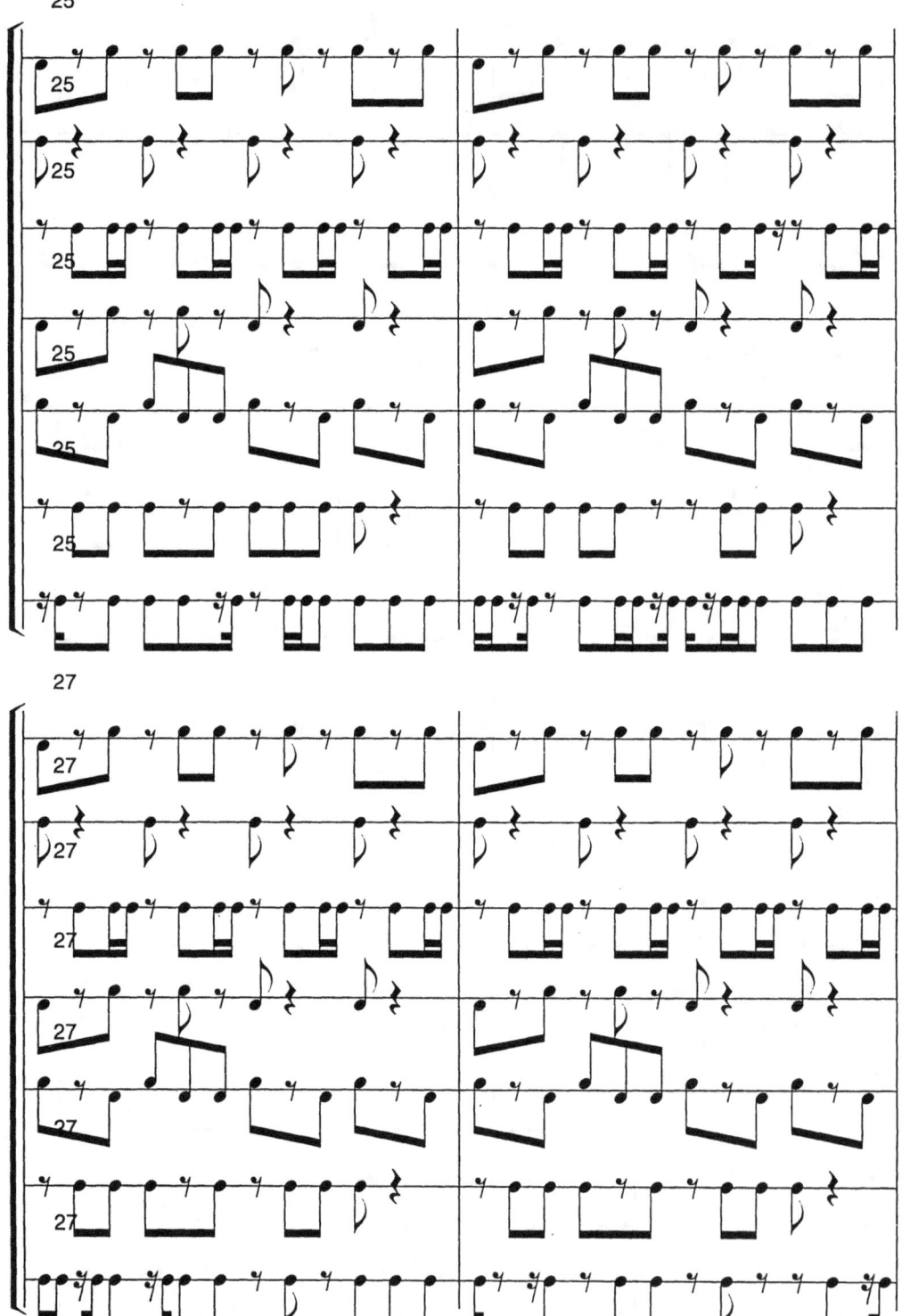

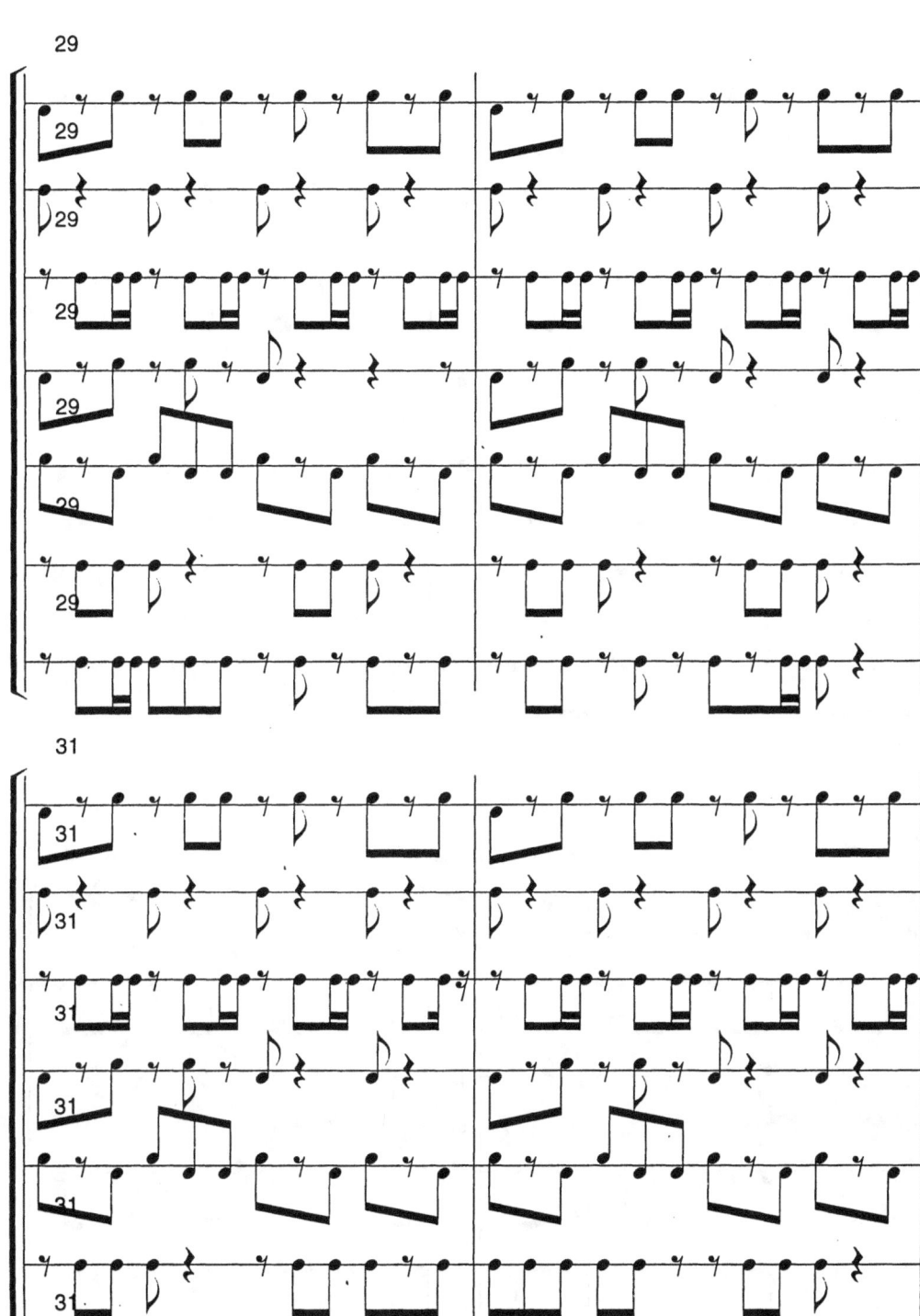

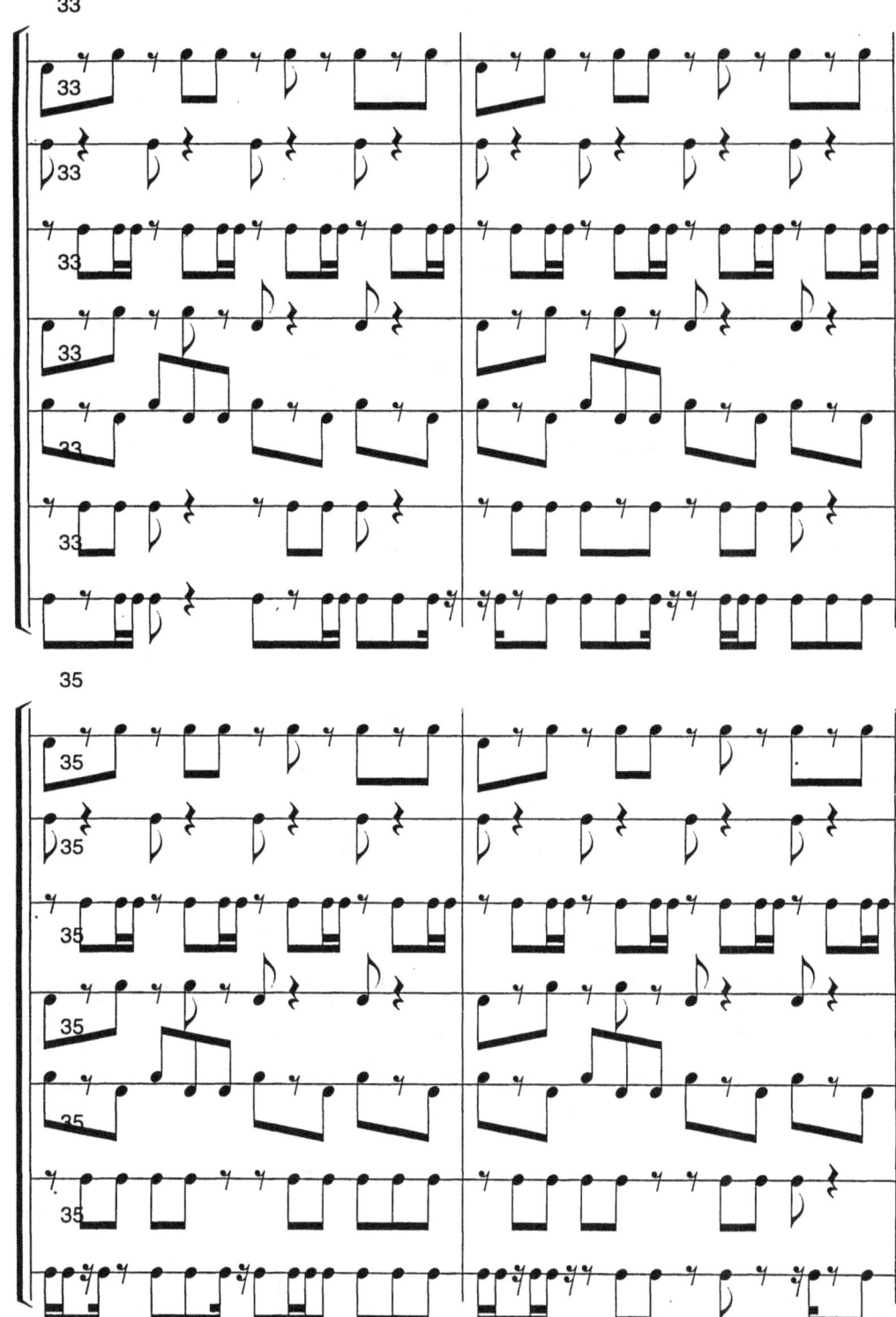

12

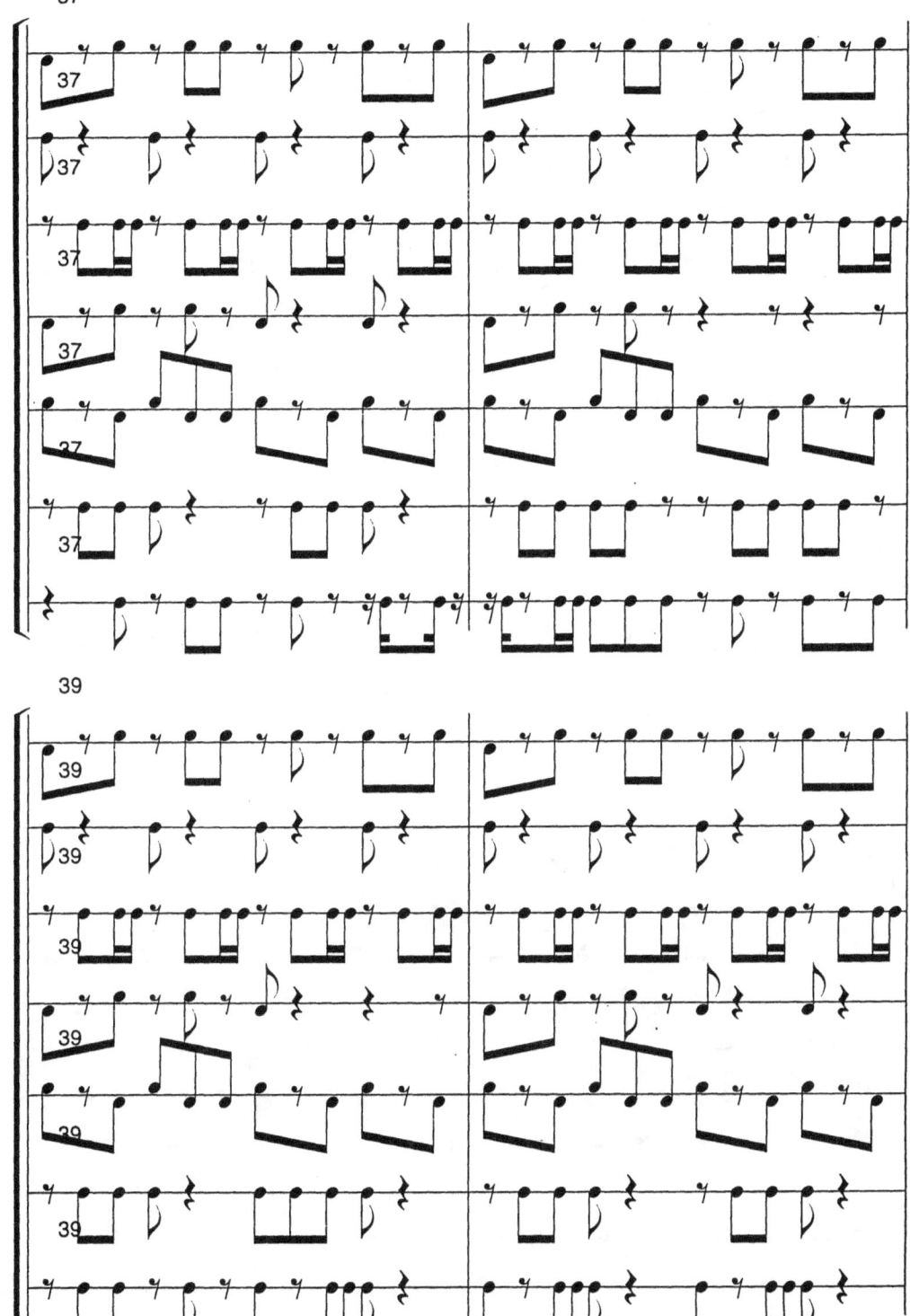

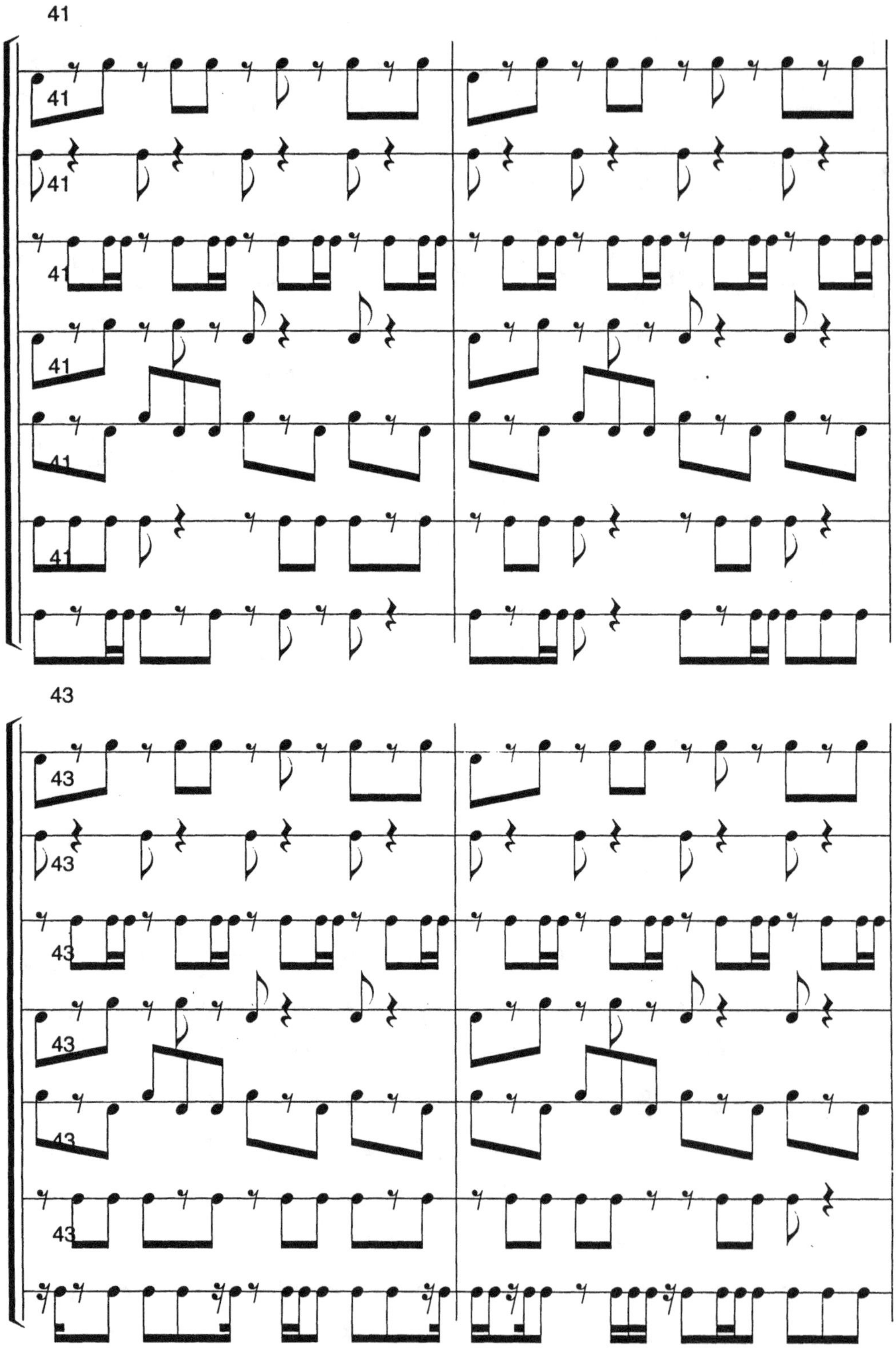

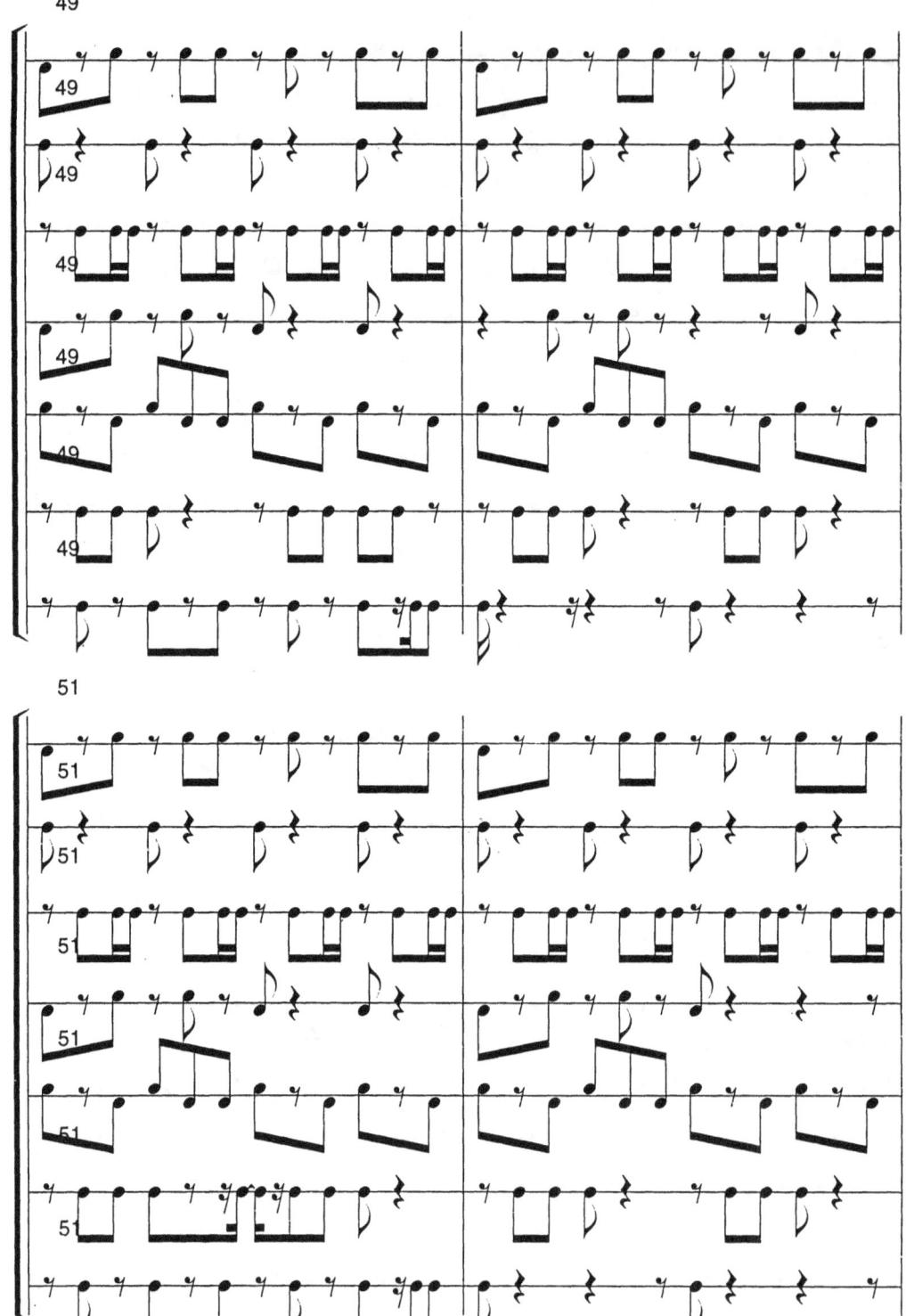

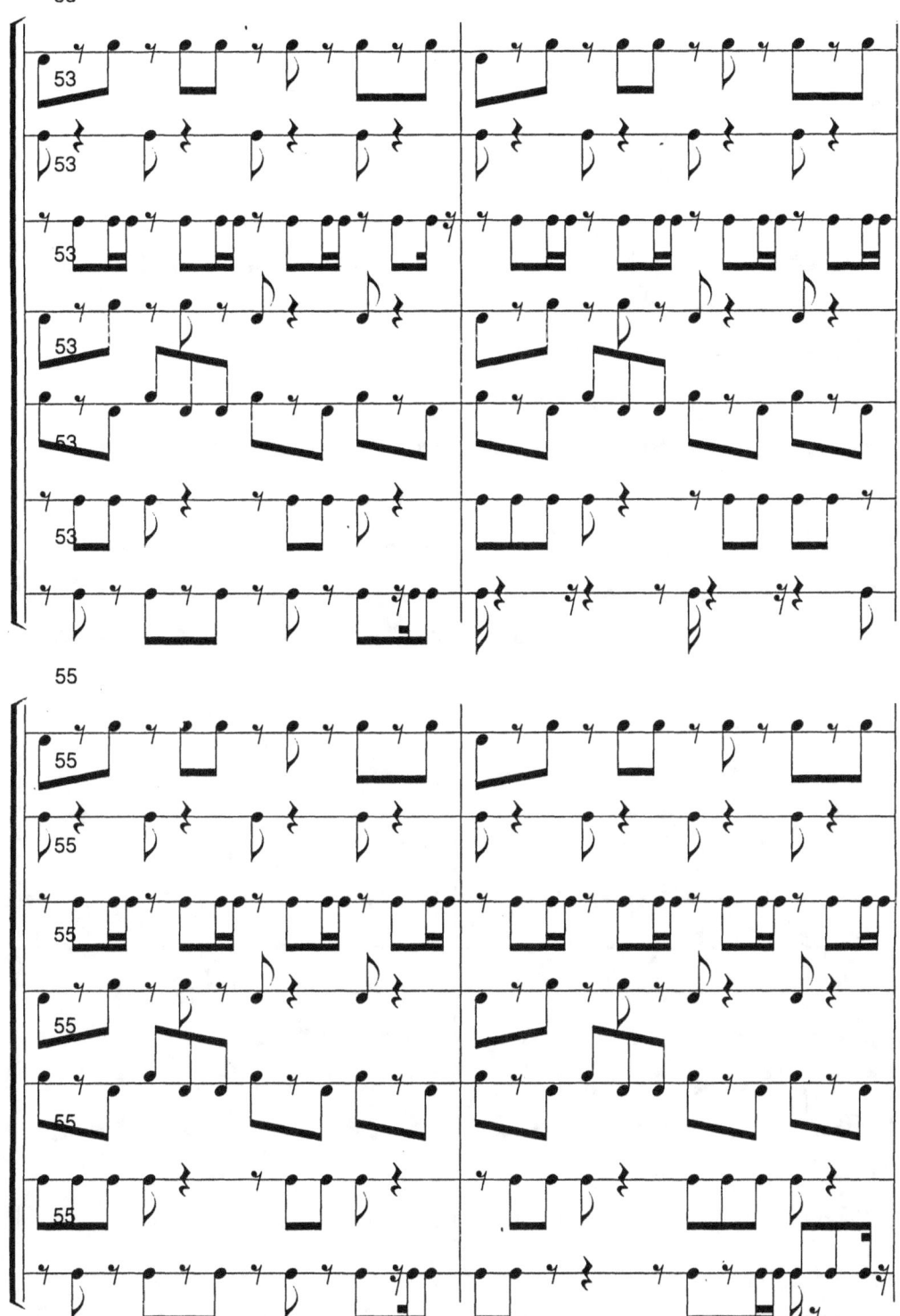

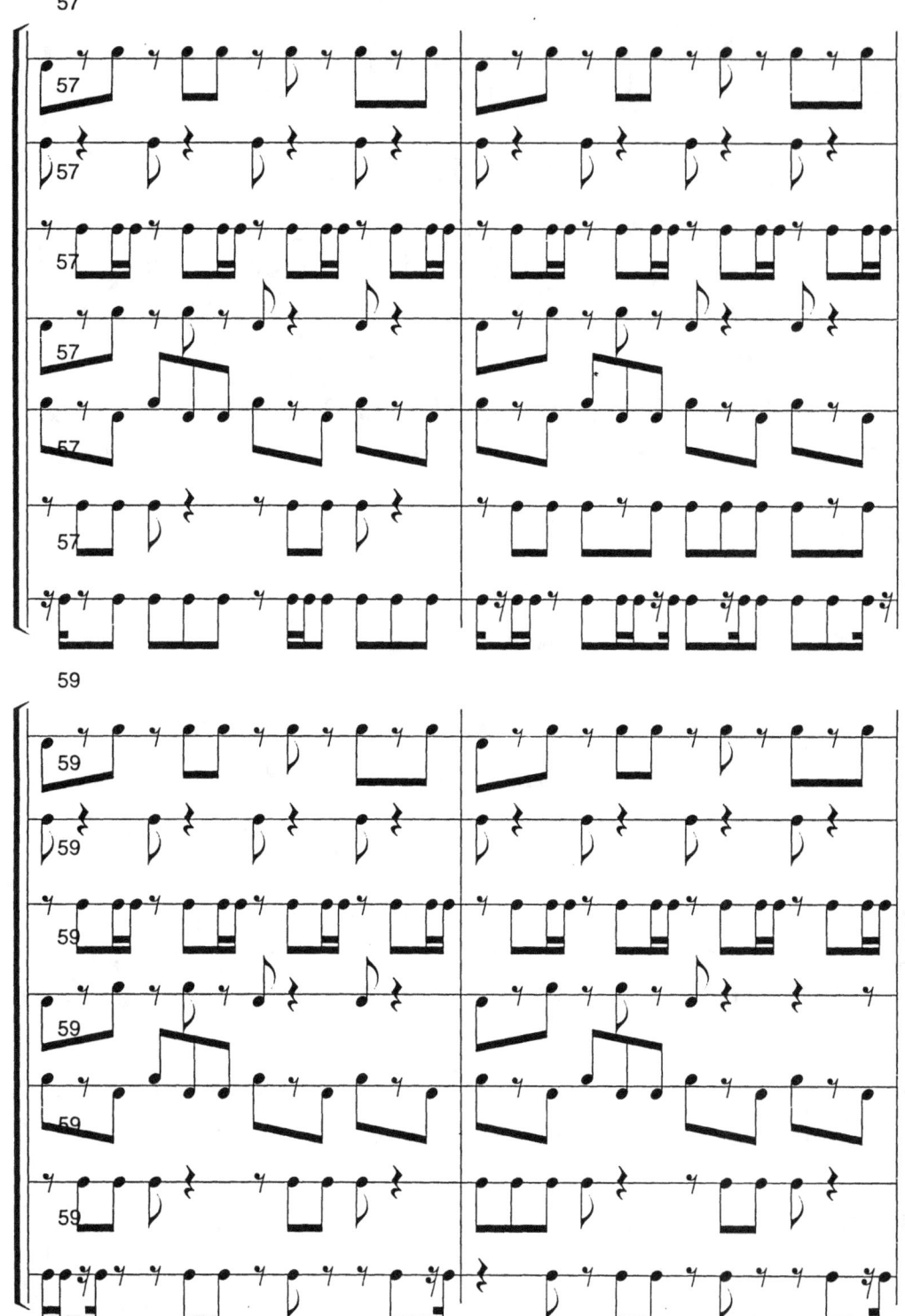

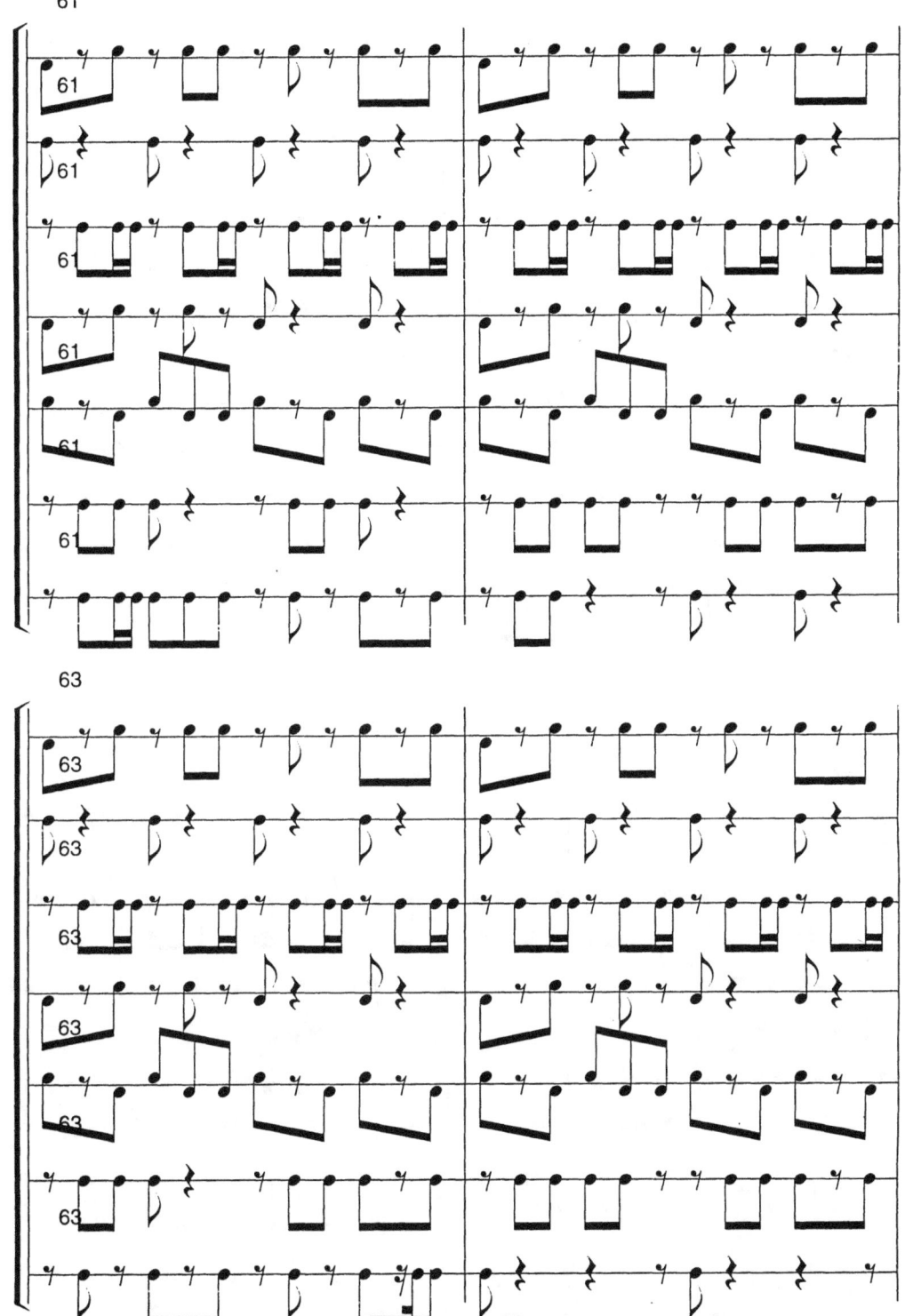

21

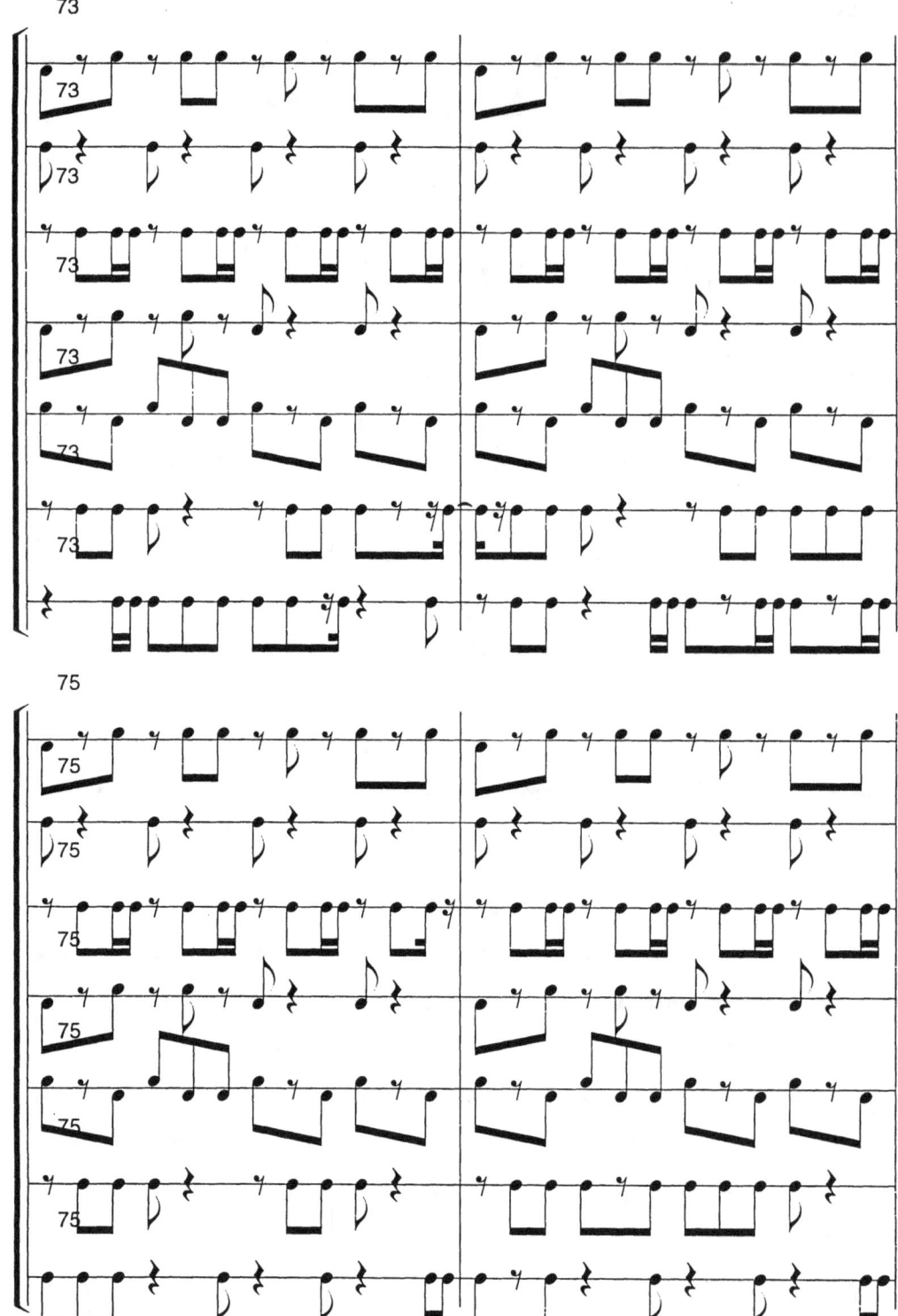

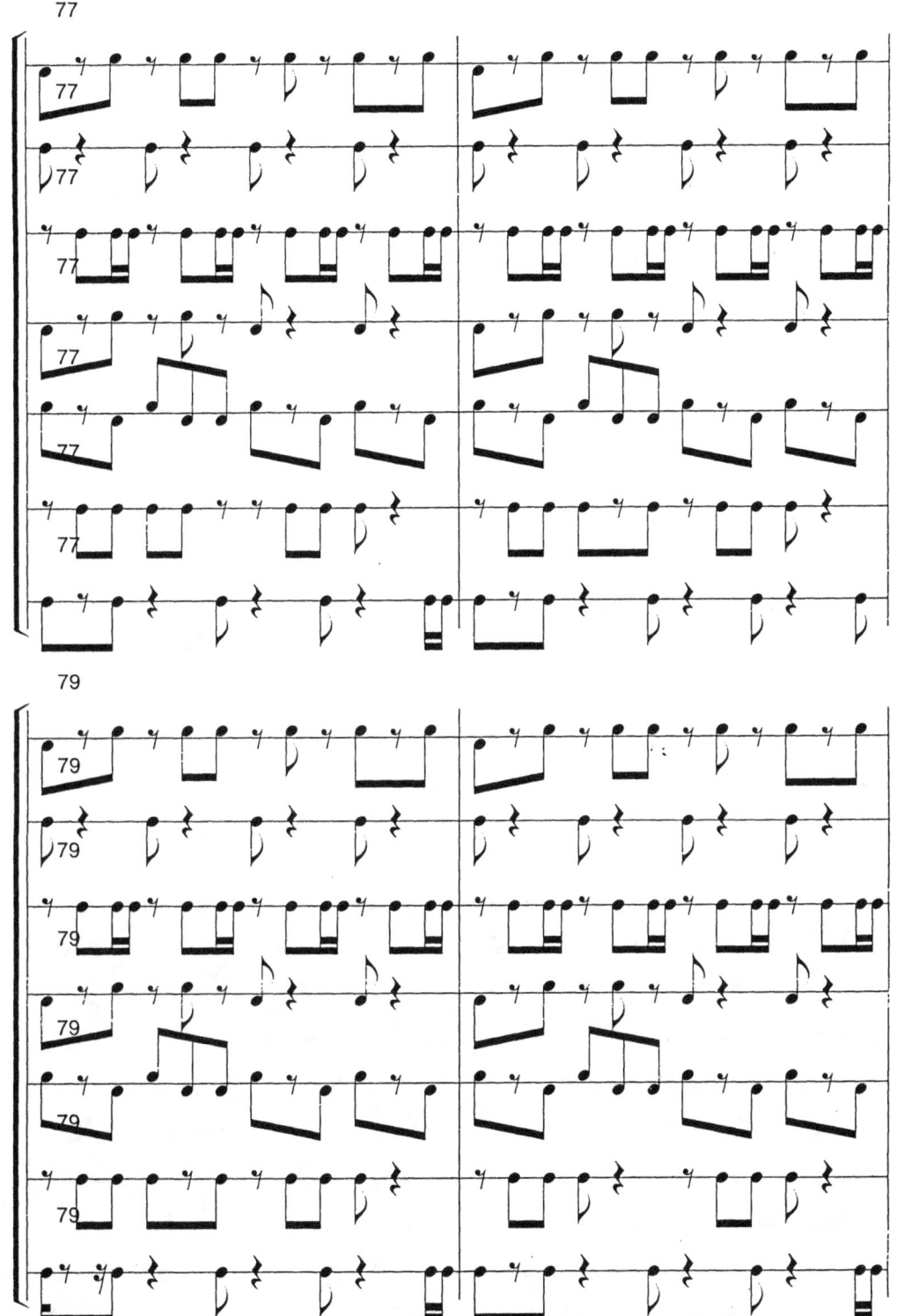

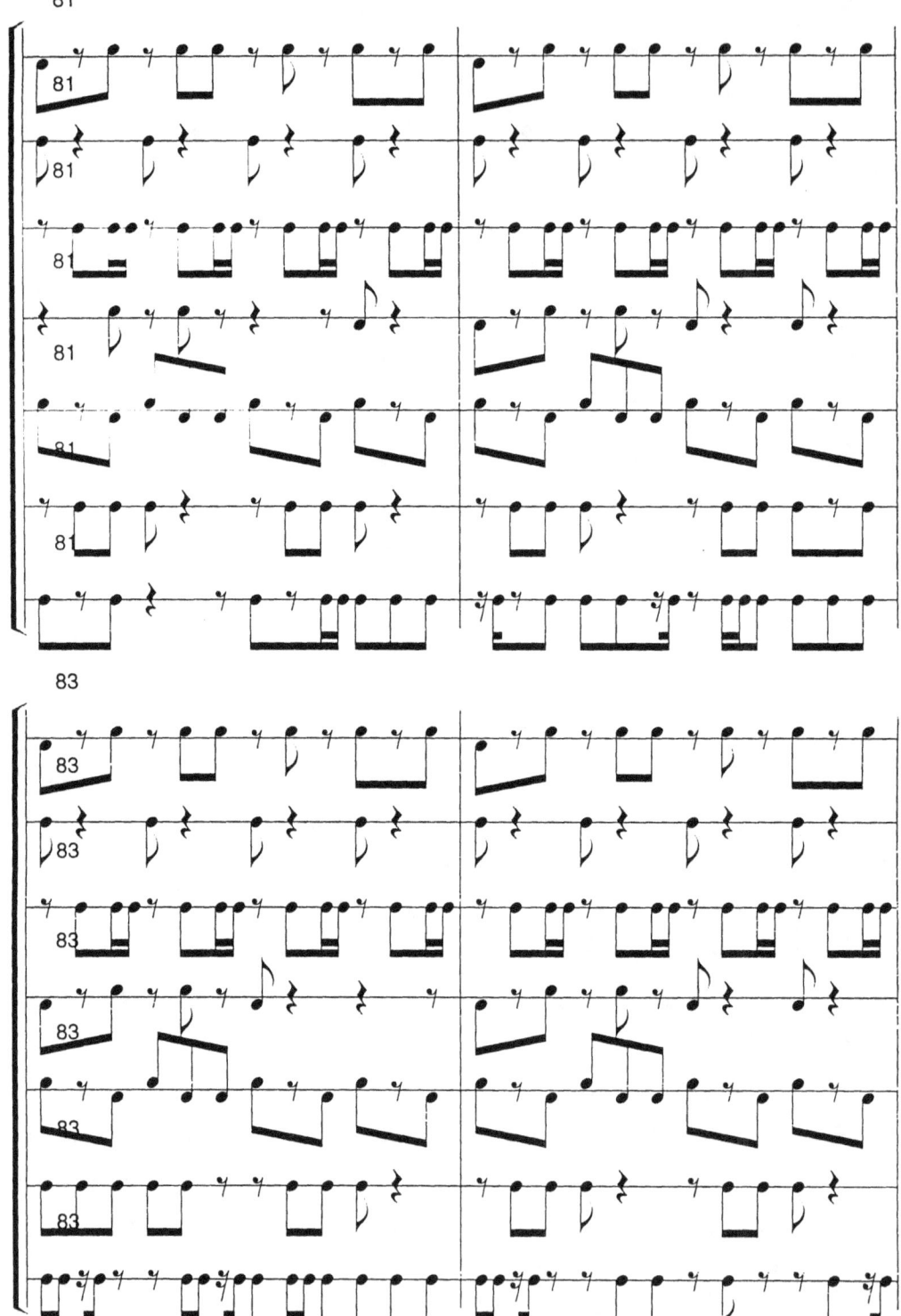

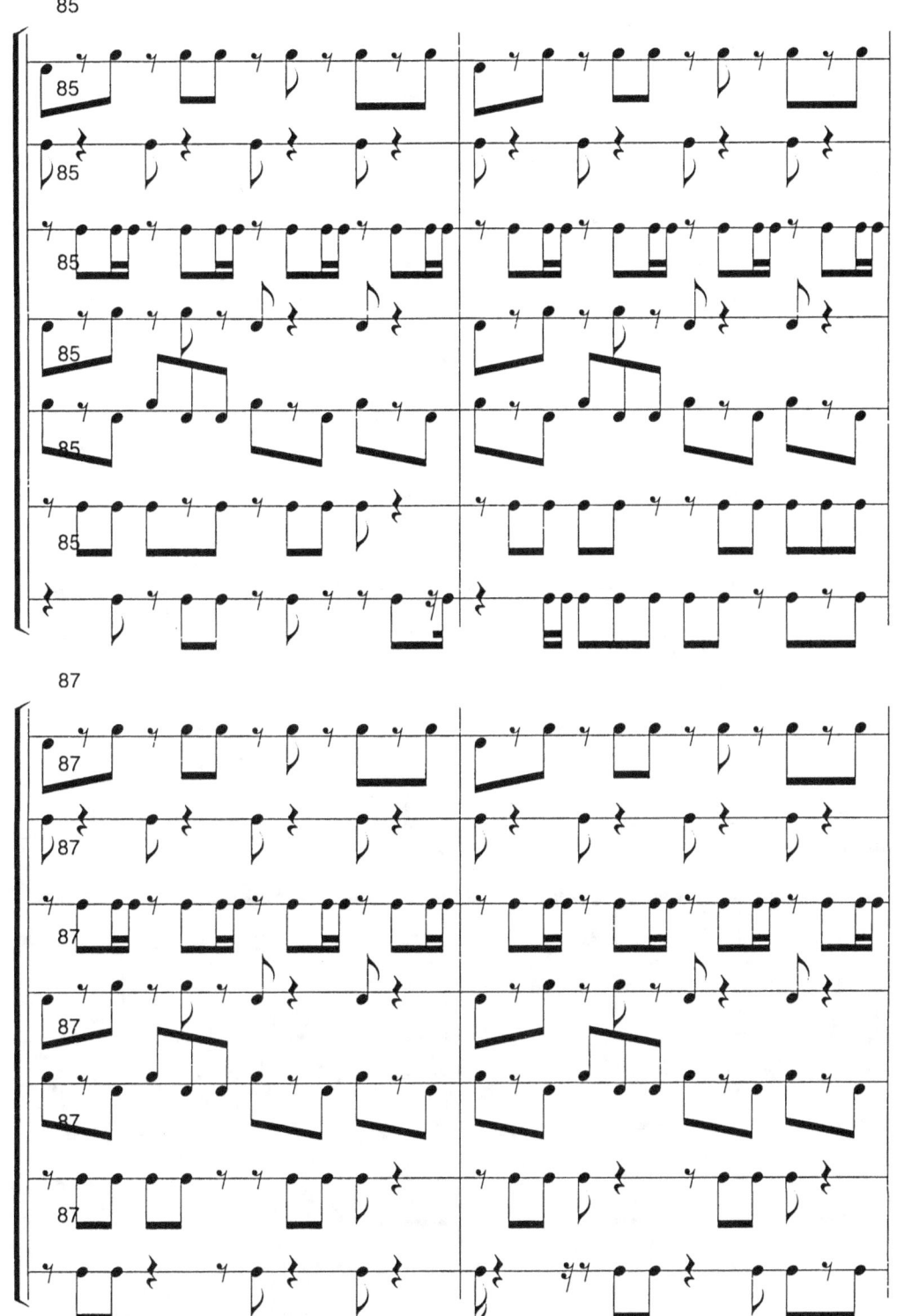

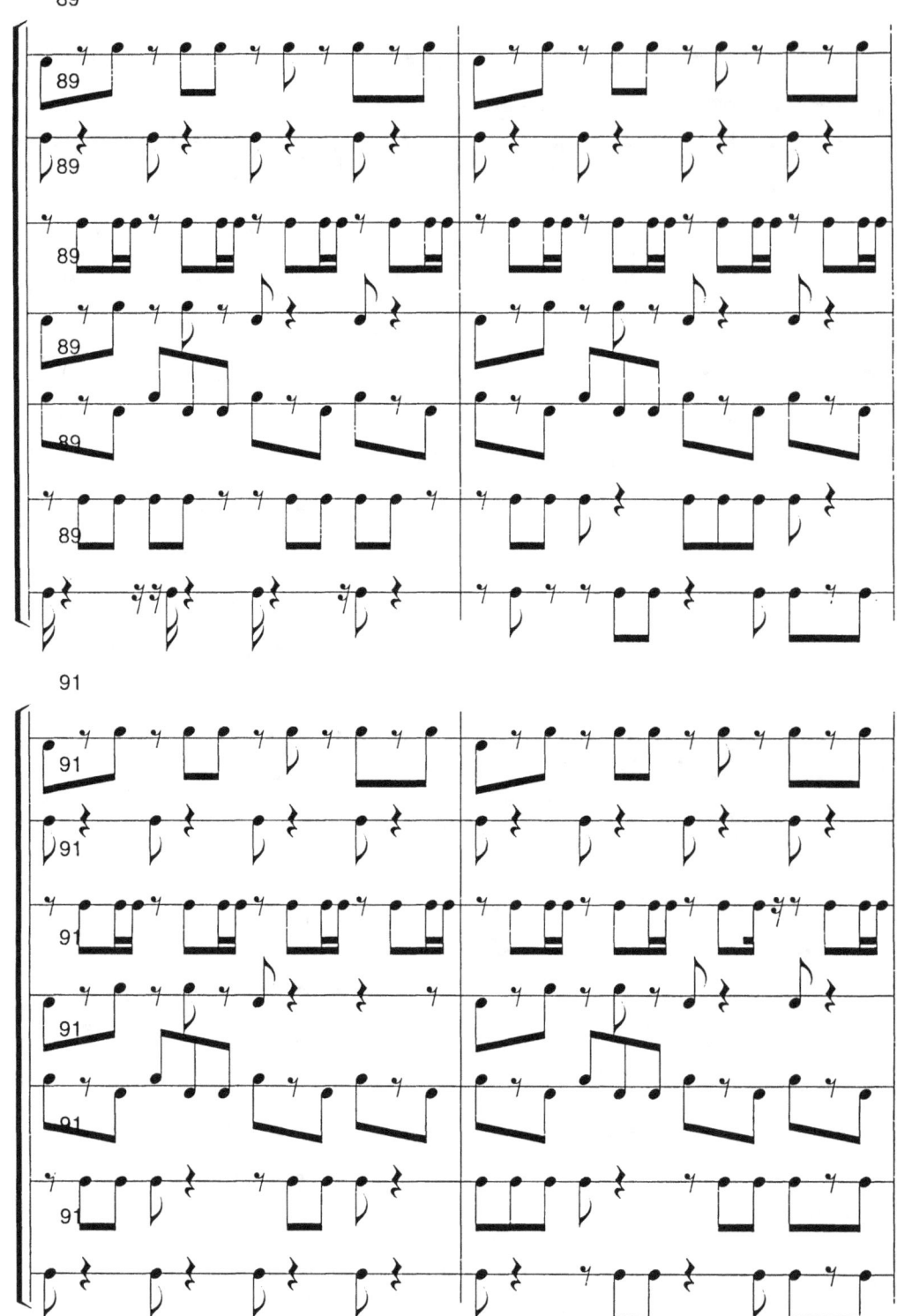

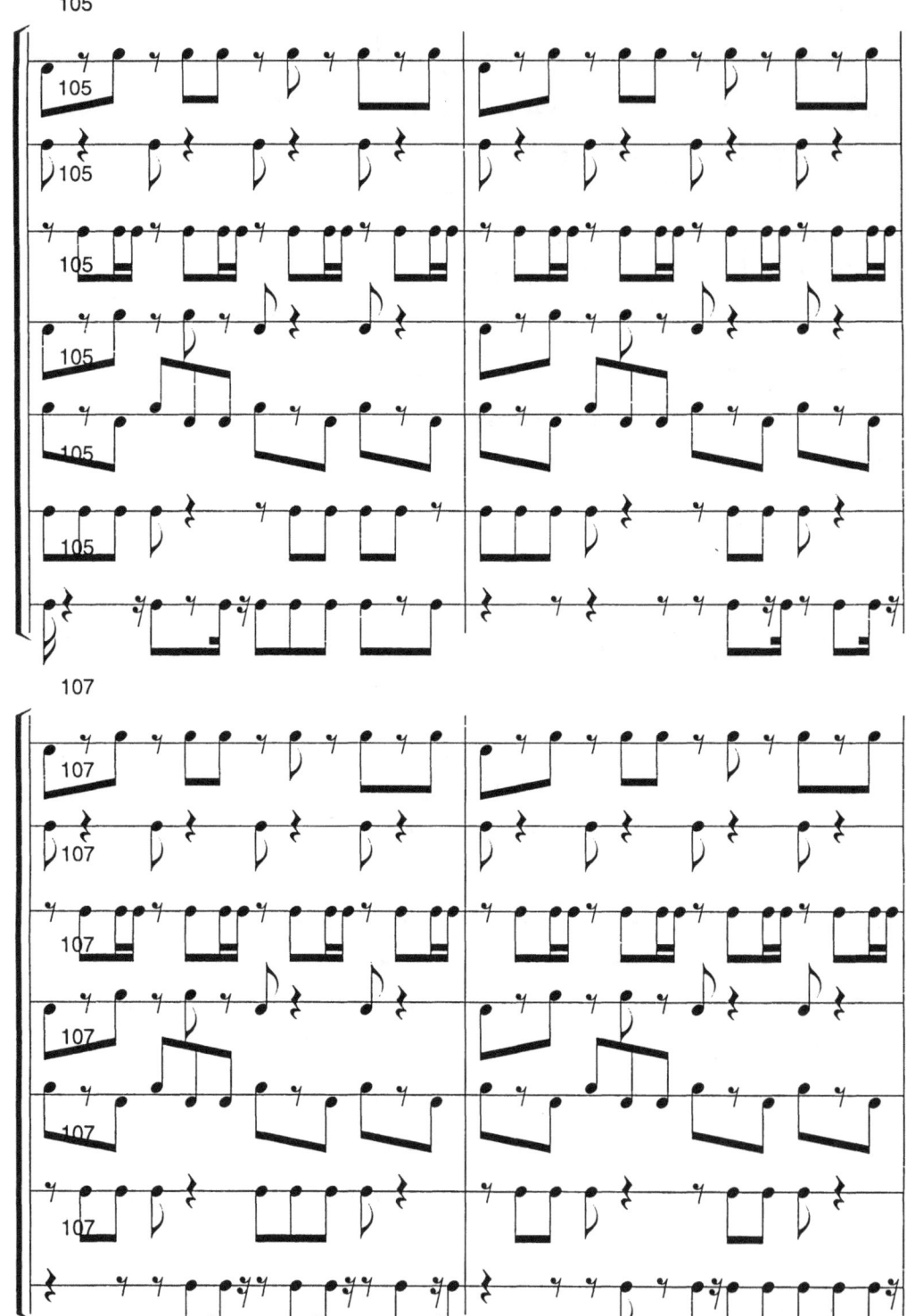

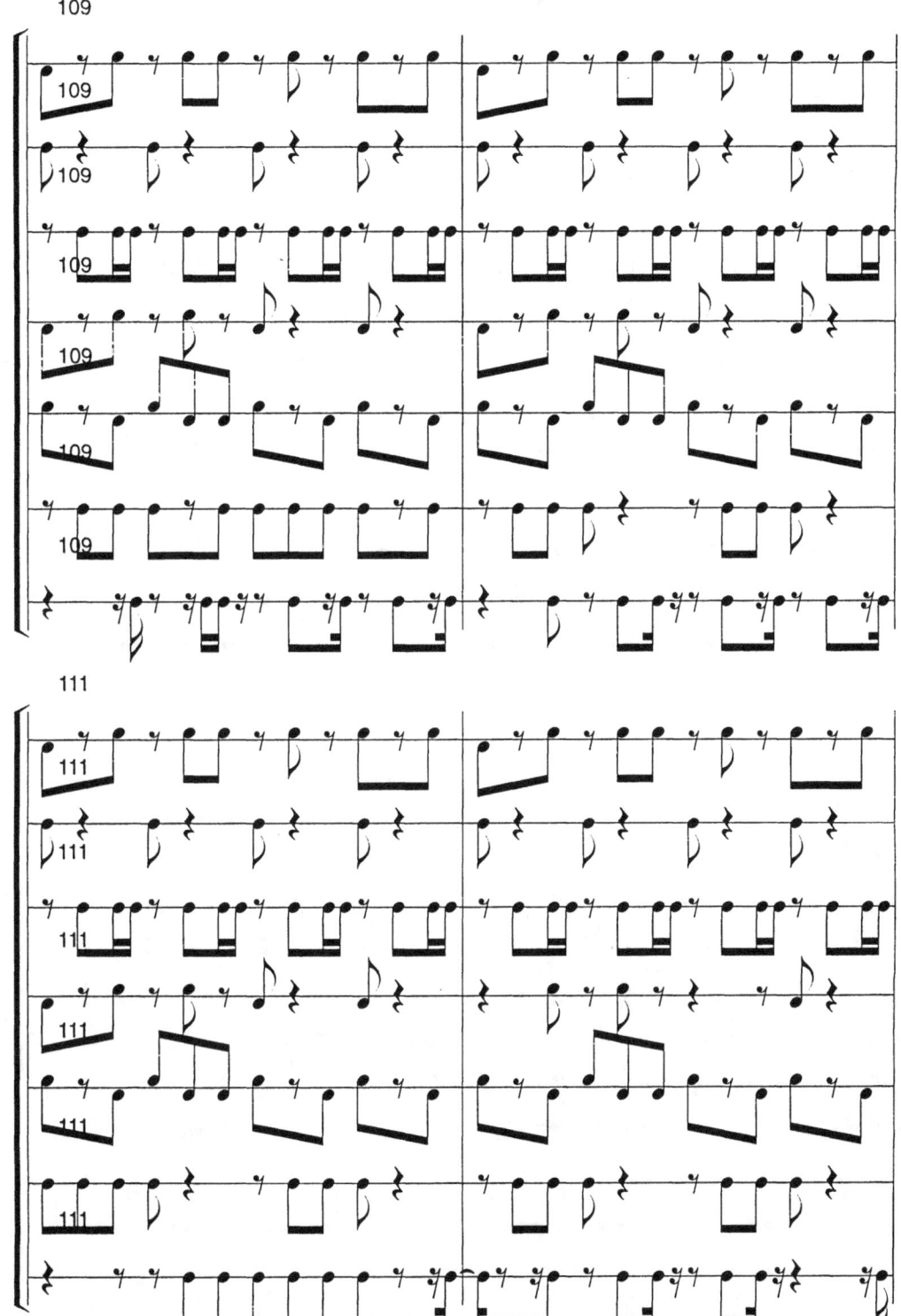

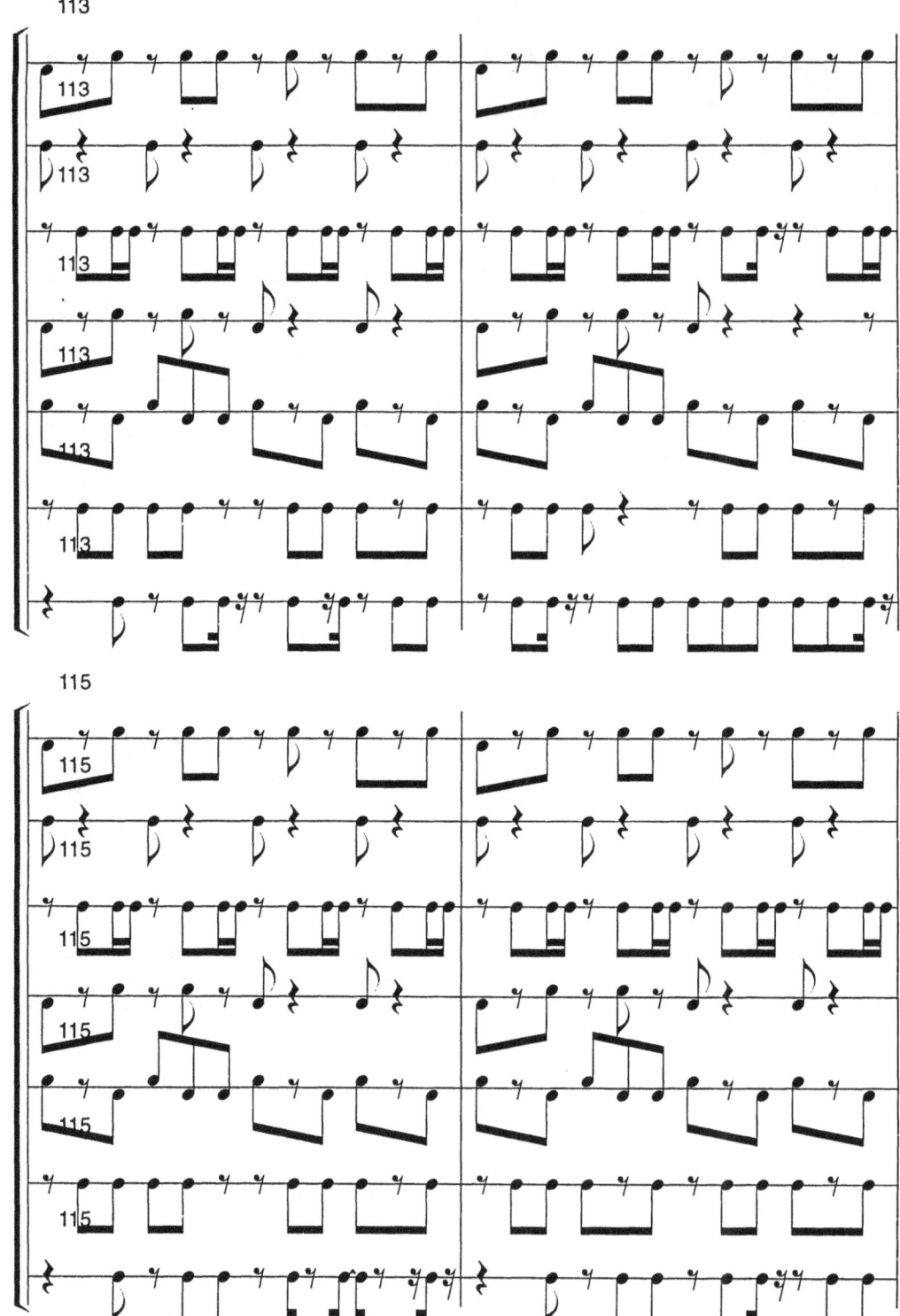

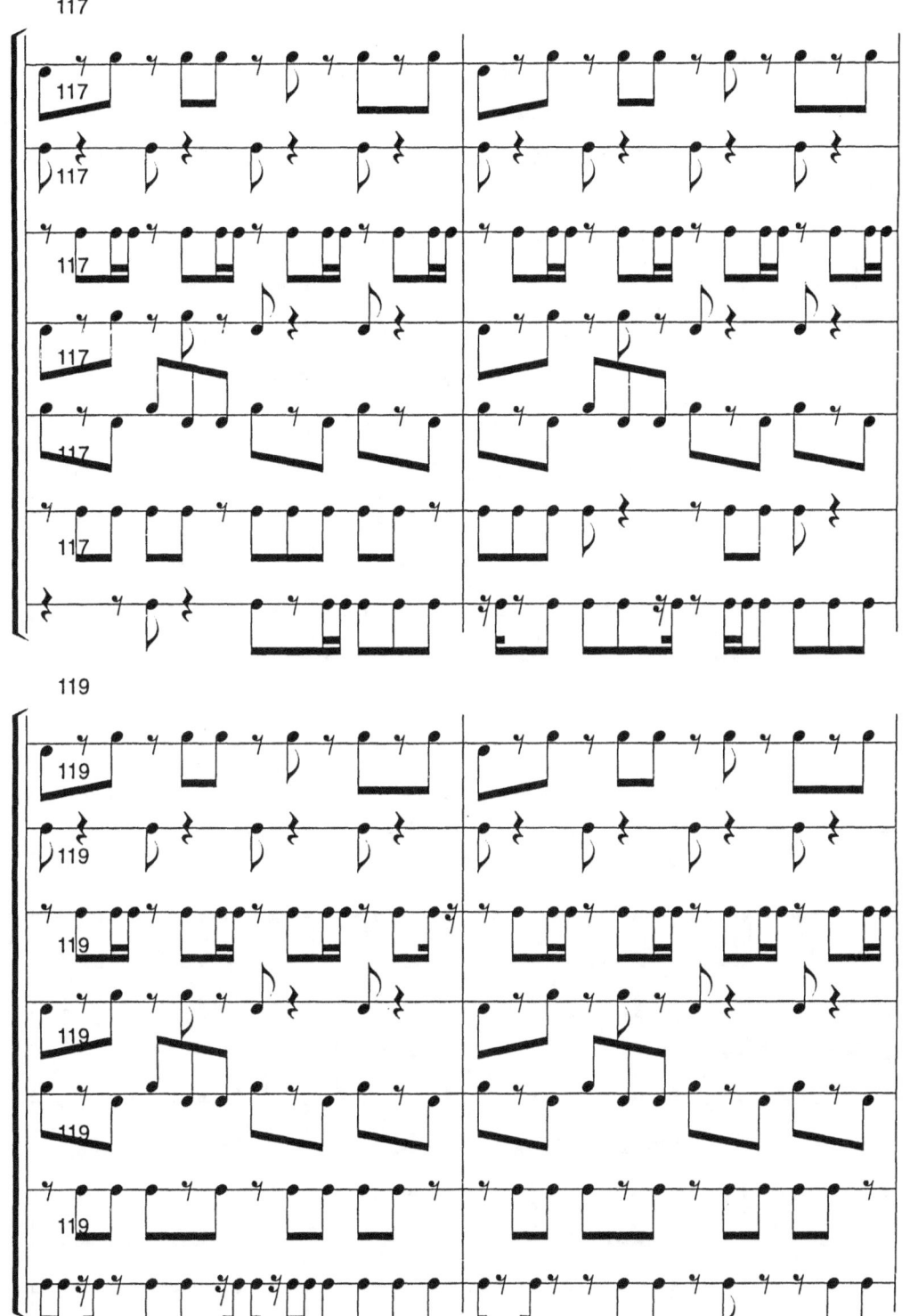

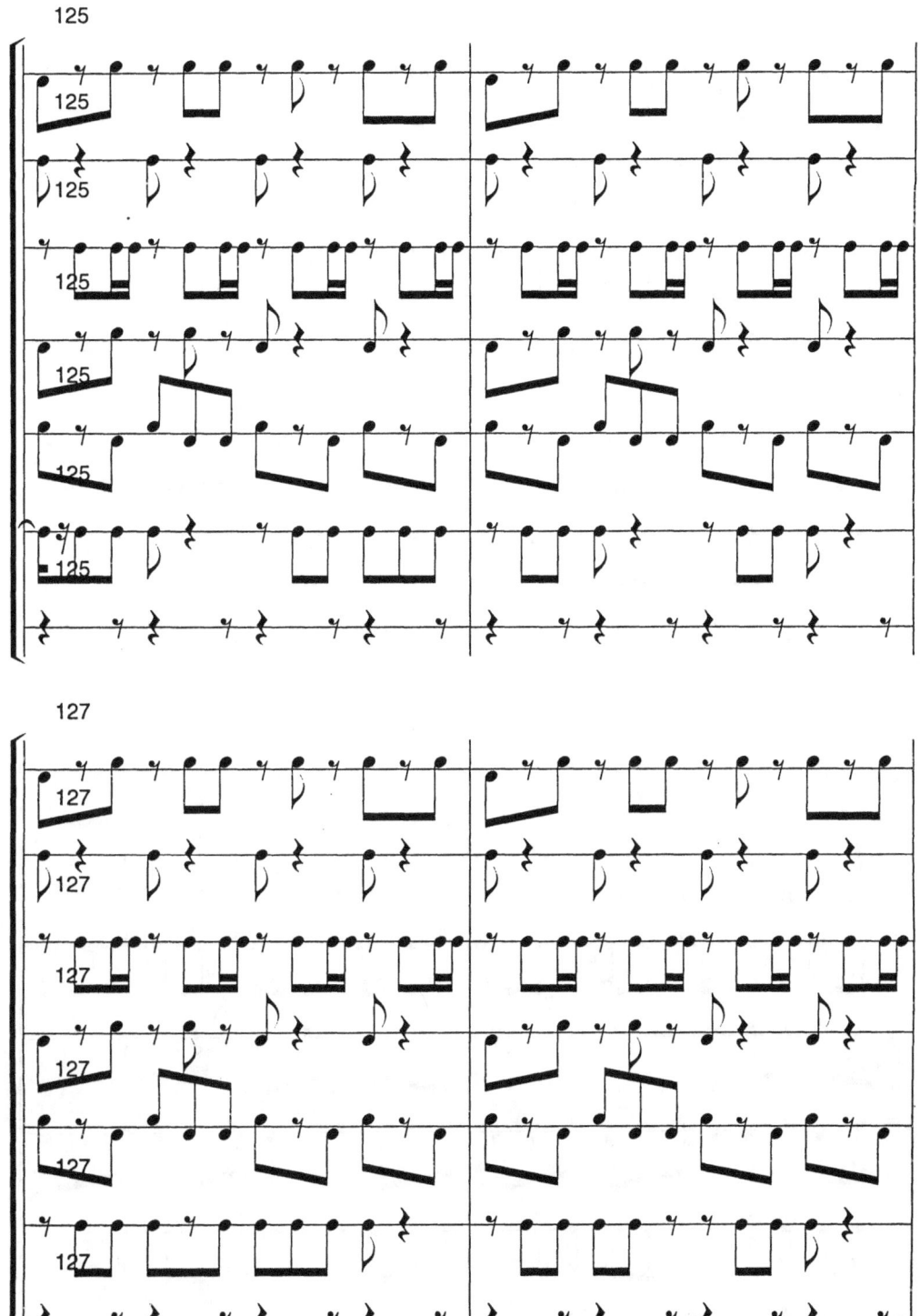

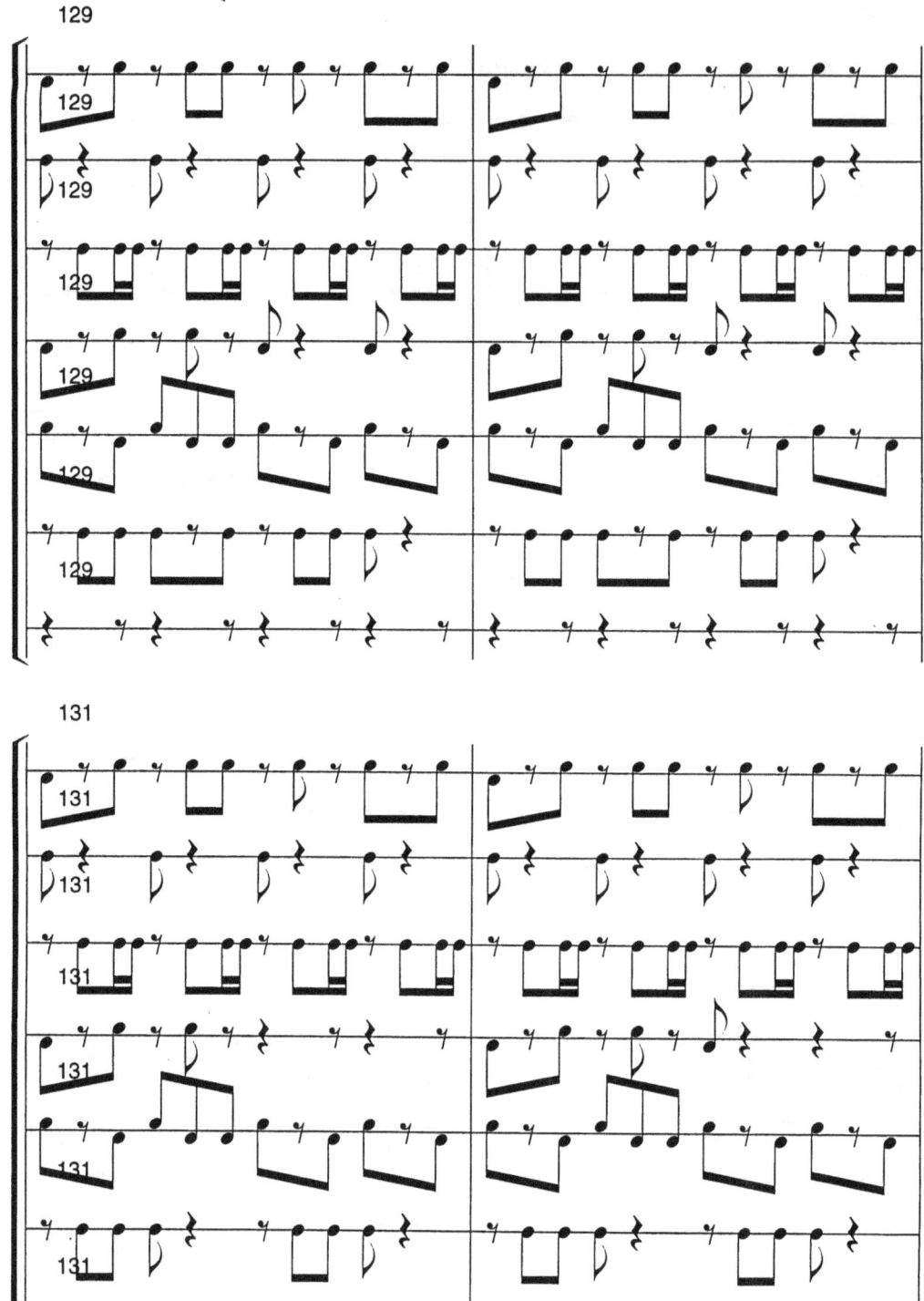

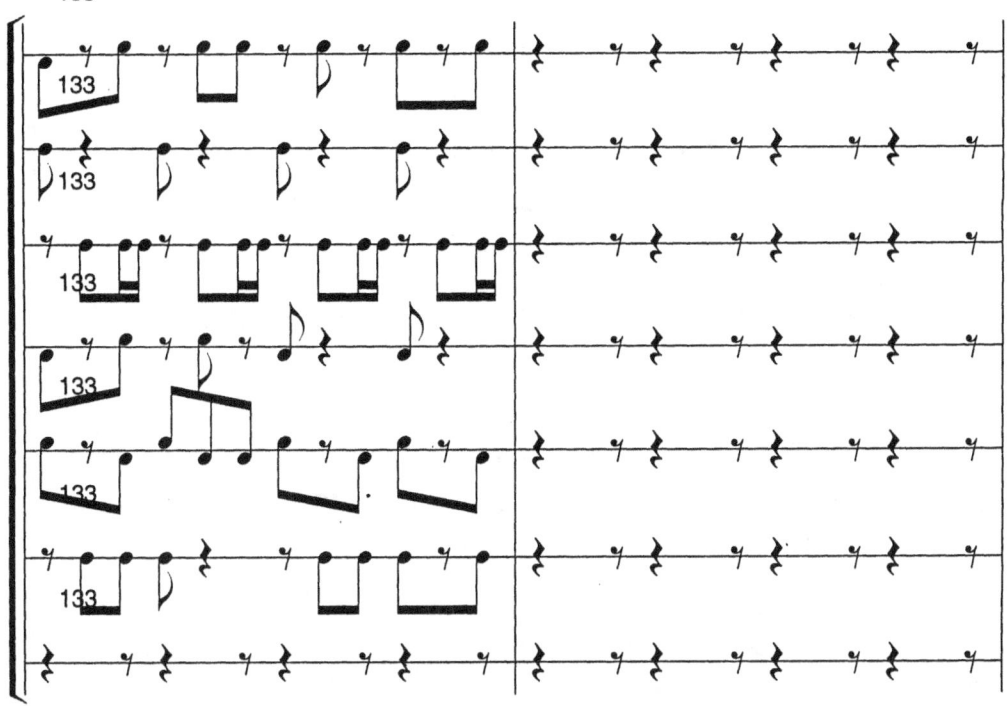

Note on Atsimevu :

For the seven first measures of Atsimevu given above, the patterns below are what some drummers play

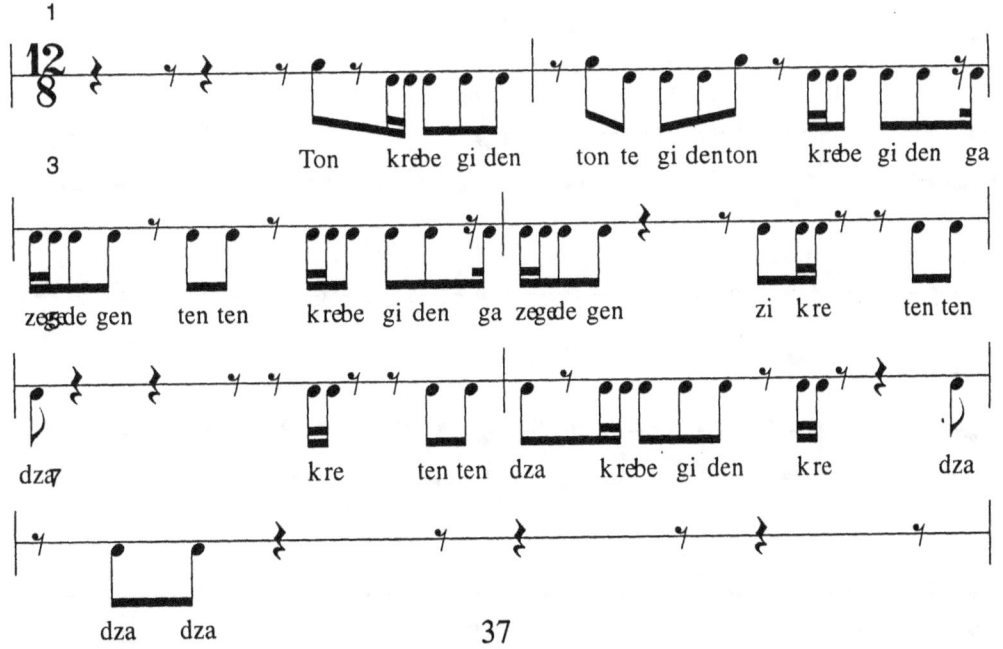

Vertical alignment
Gakogui and axatse

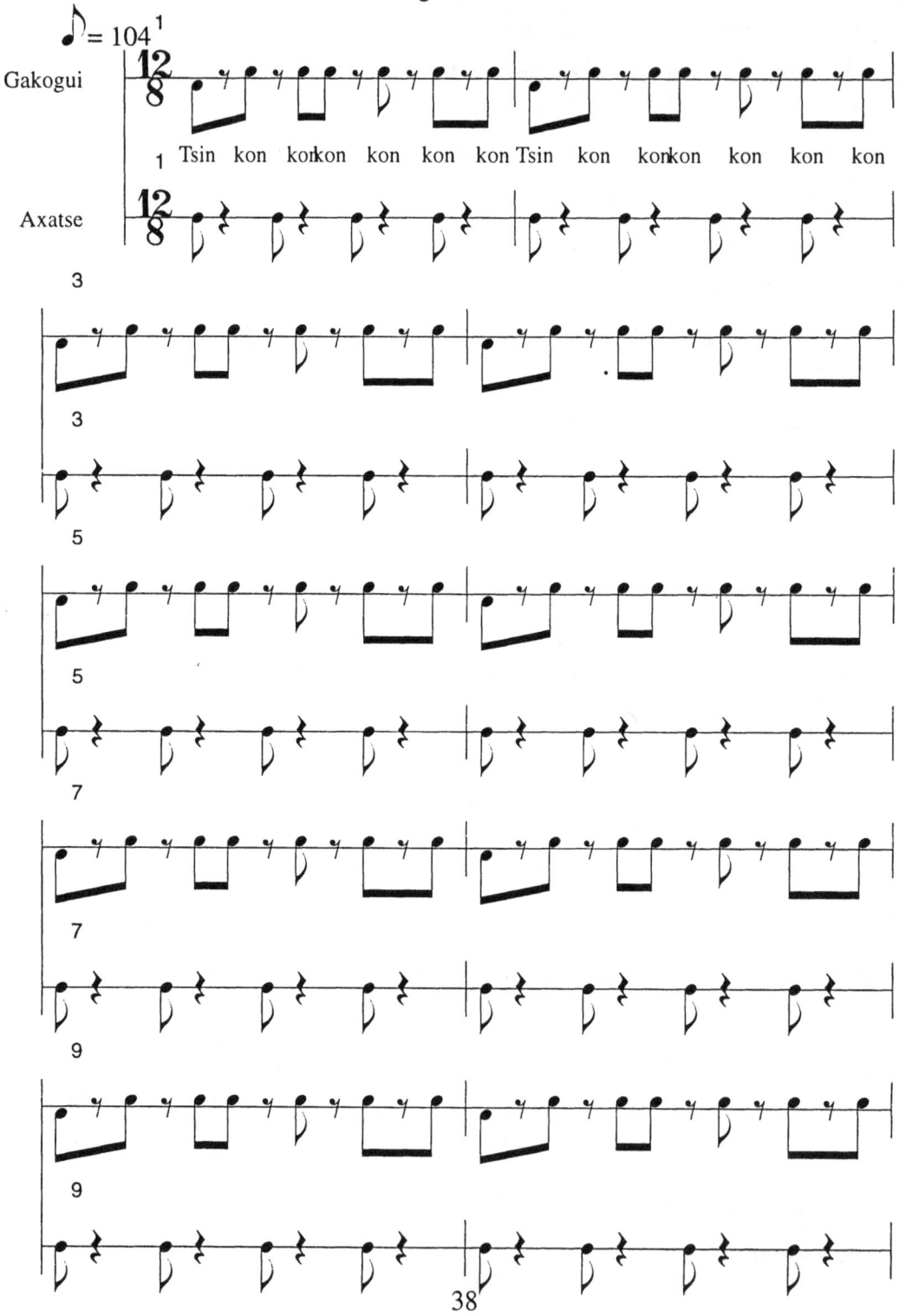

Gakogui and kagan

Gakogui and totodzi

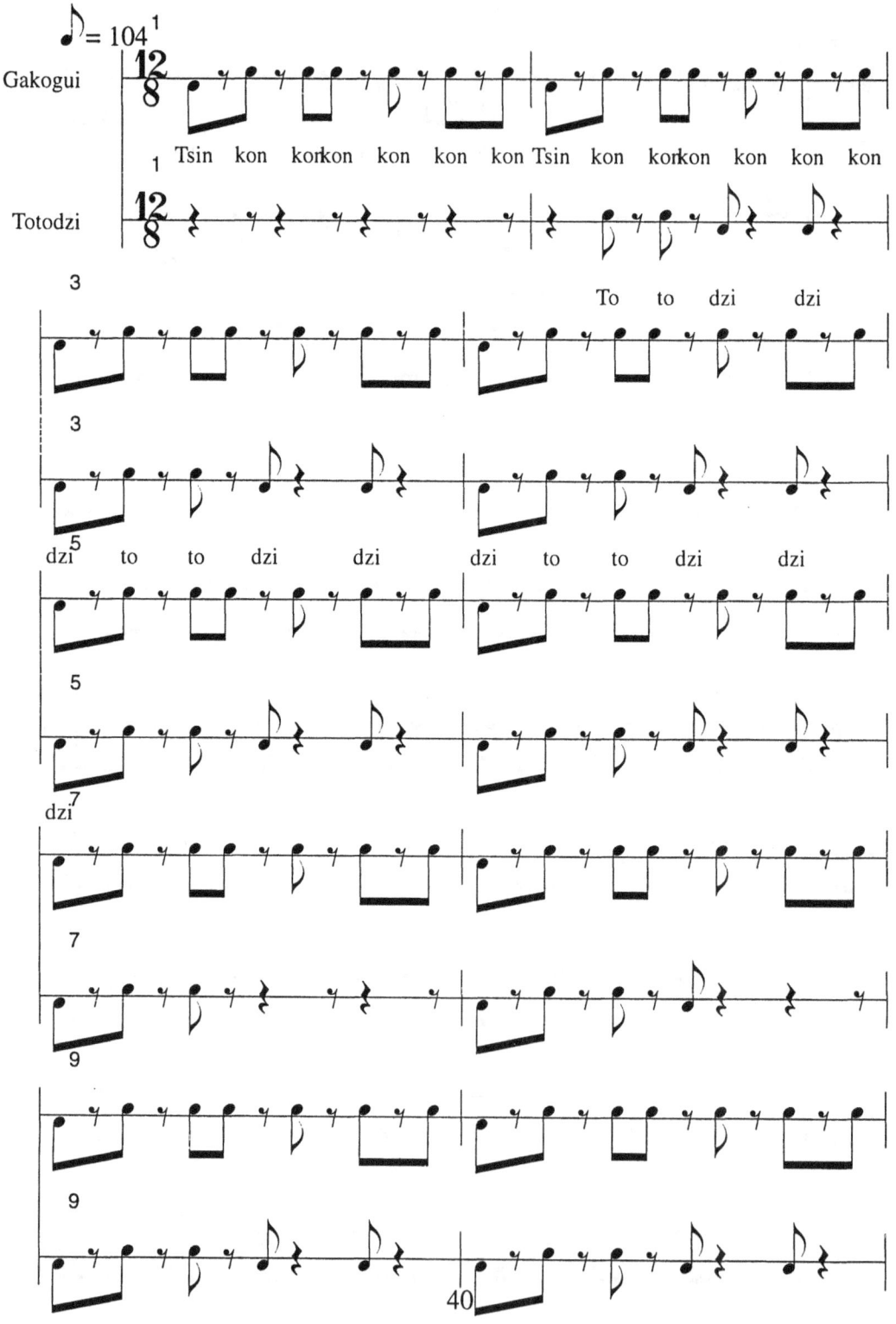

Gakogui and kroboto

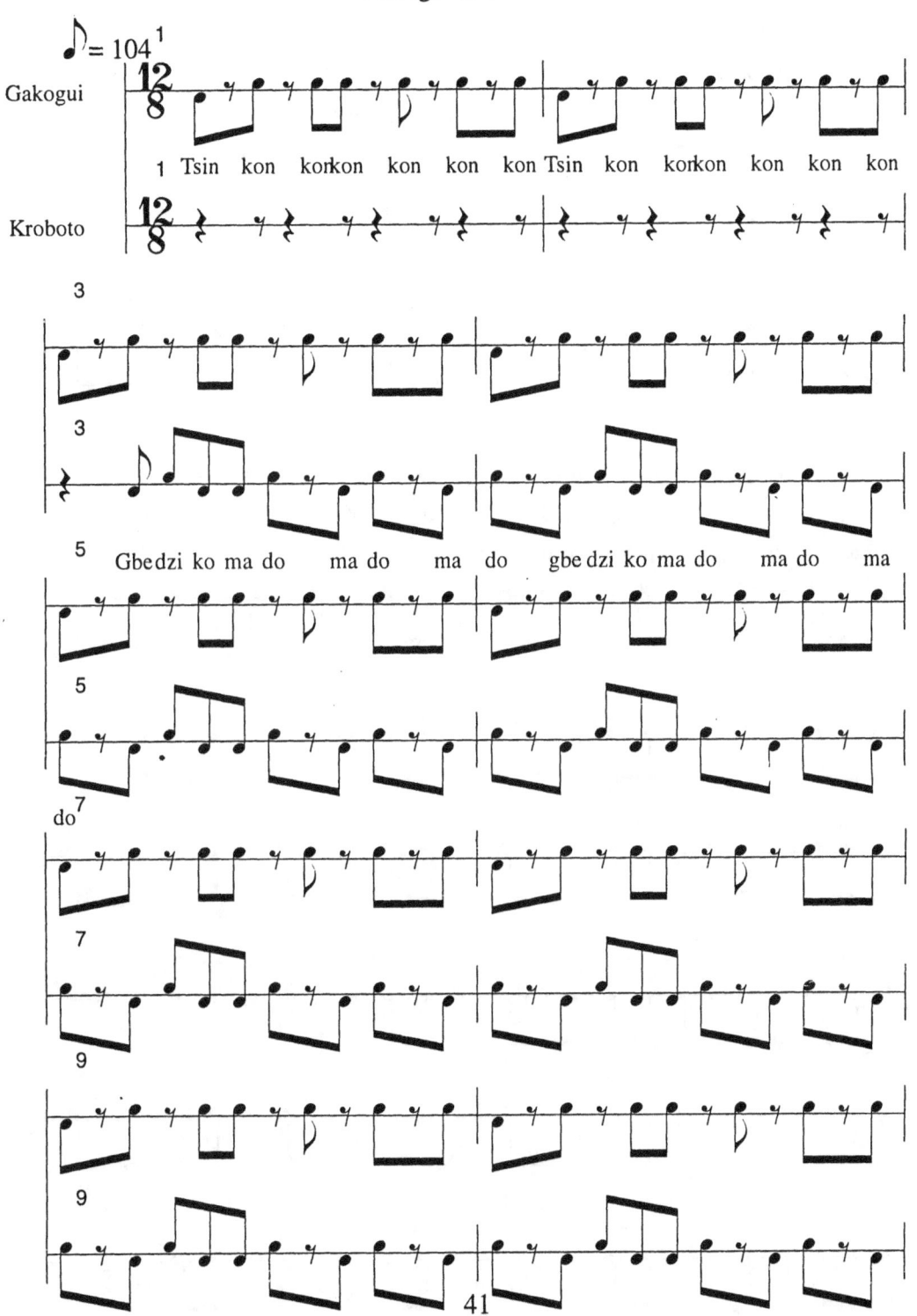

Gakogui and kidi

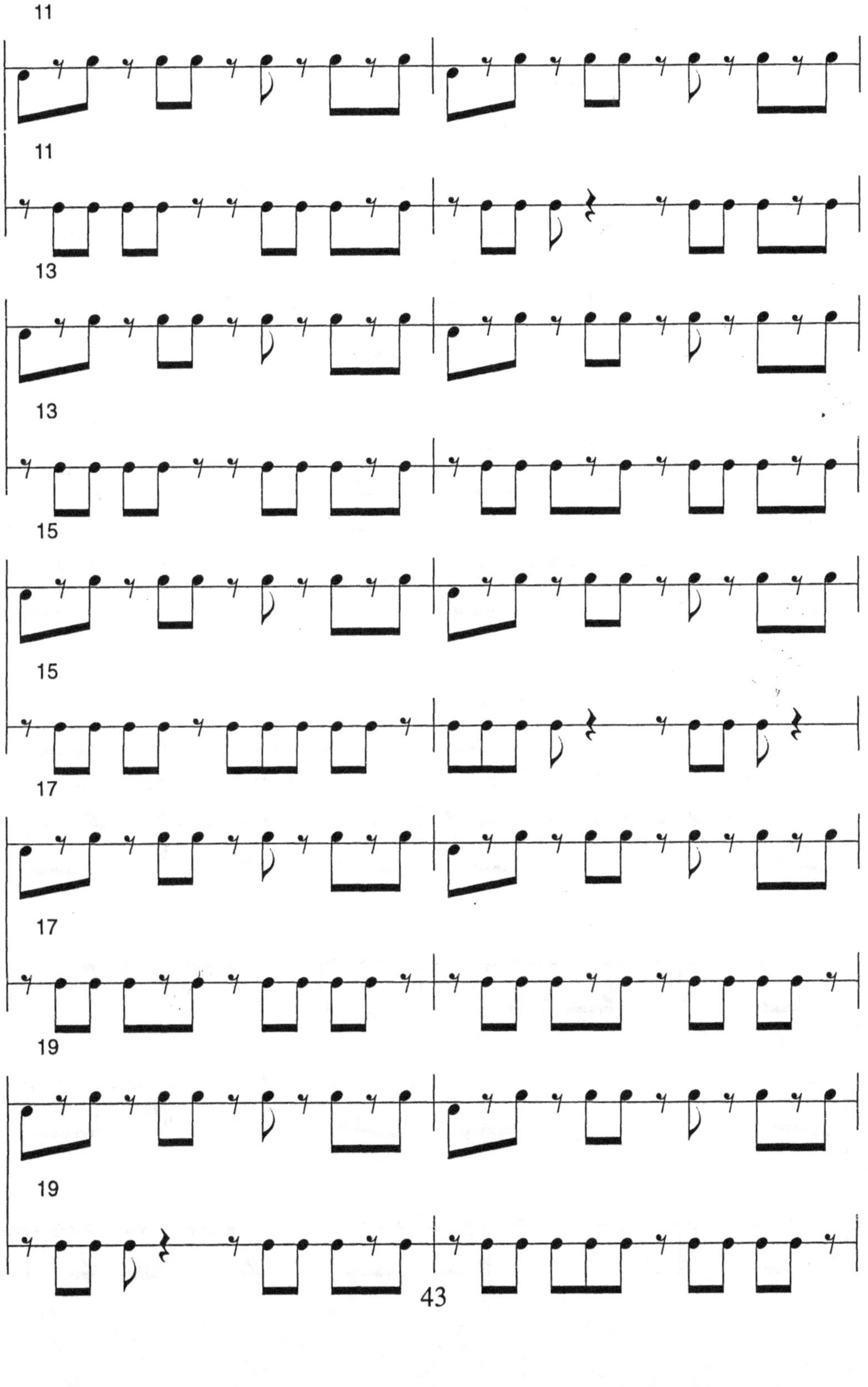
11
11
13
13
15
15
17
17
19
19

6. Gakogui and Atsimevu

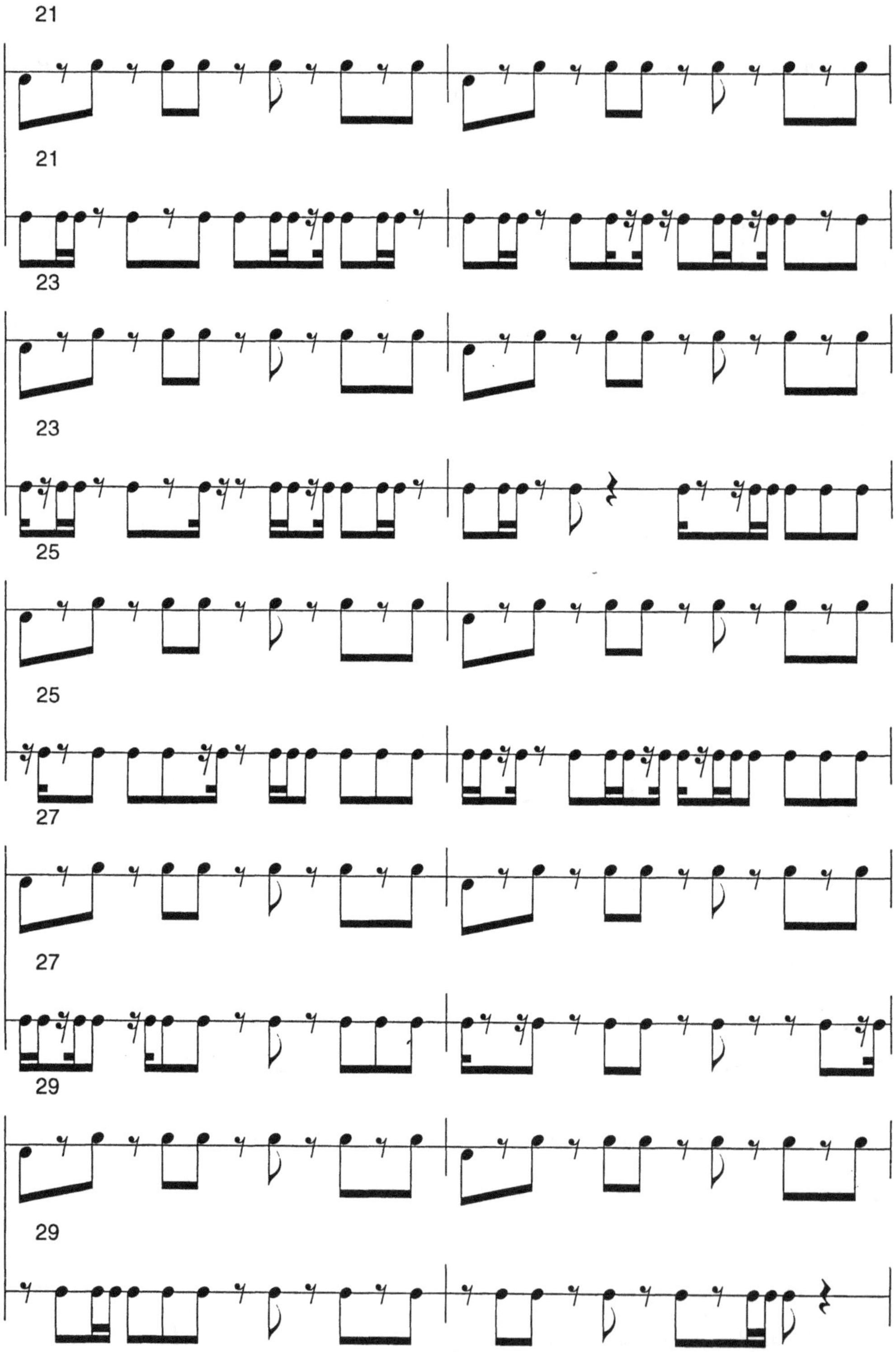
21
21
23
23
25
25
27
27
29
29

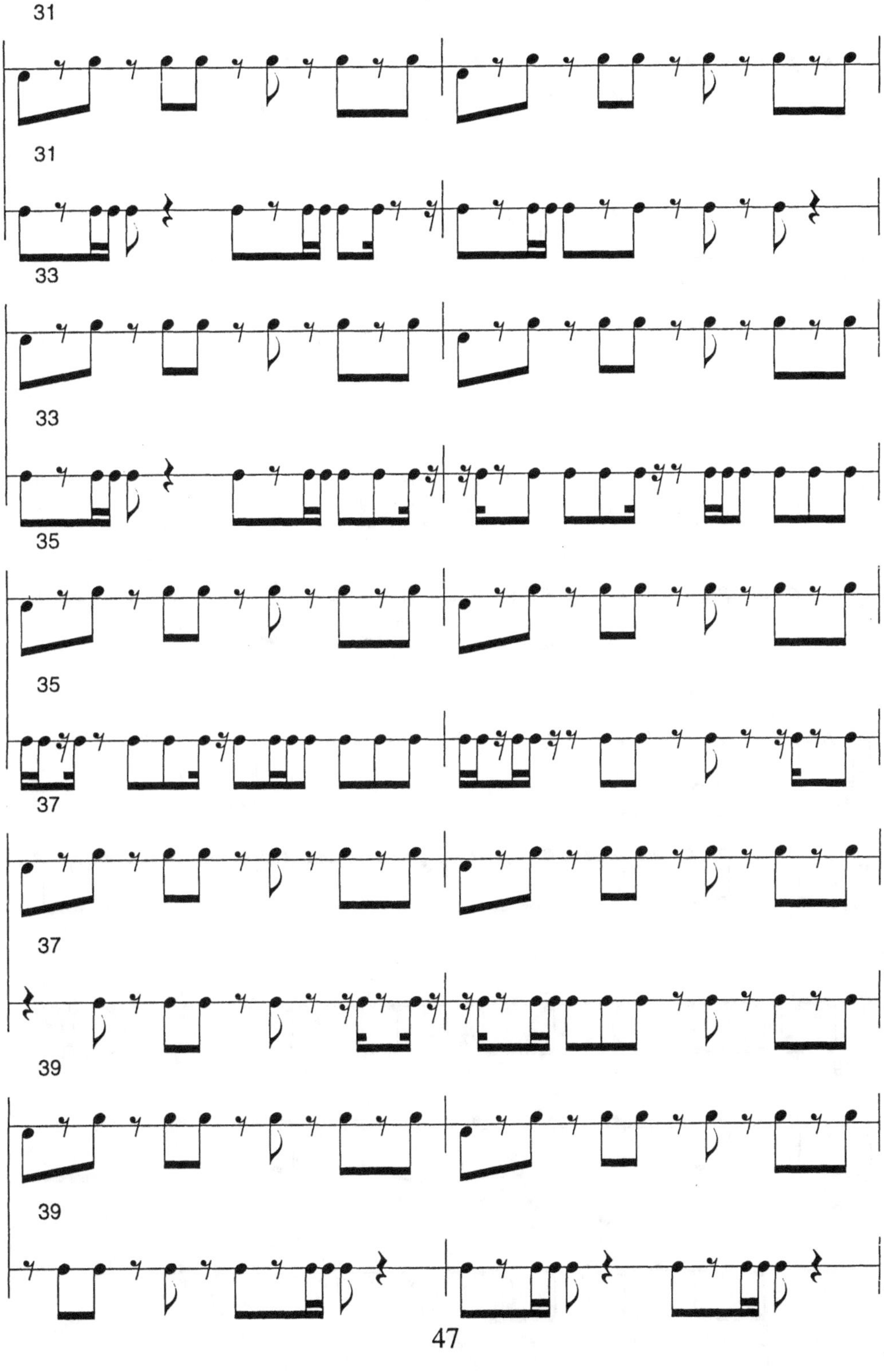
31
31
33
33
35
35
37
37
39
39

41
41
43
43
45
45
47
47
49
49

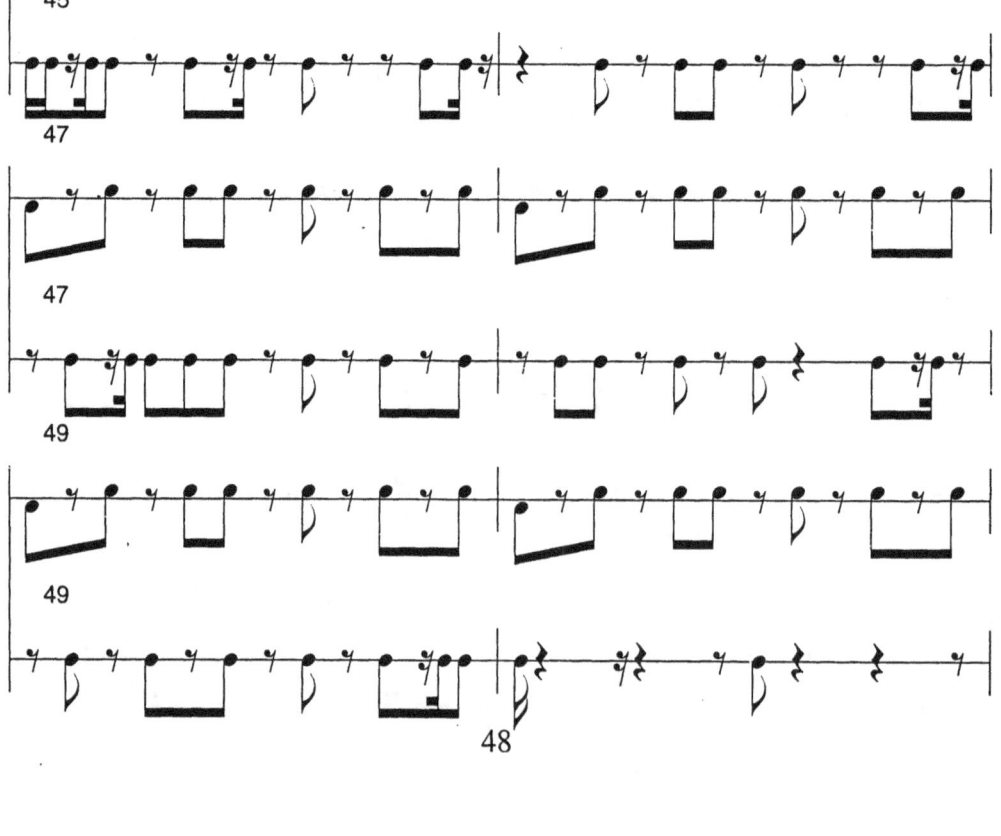

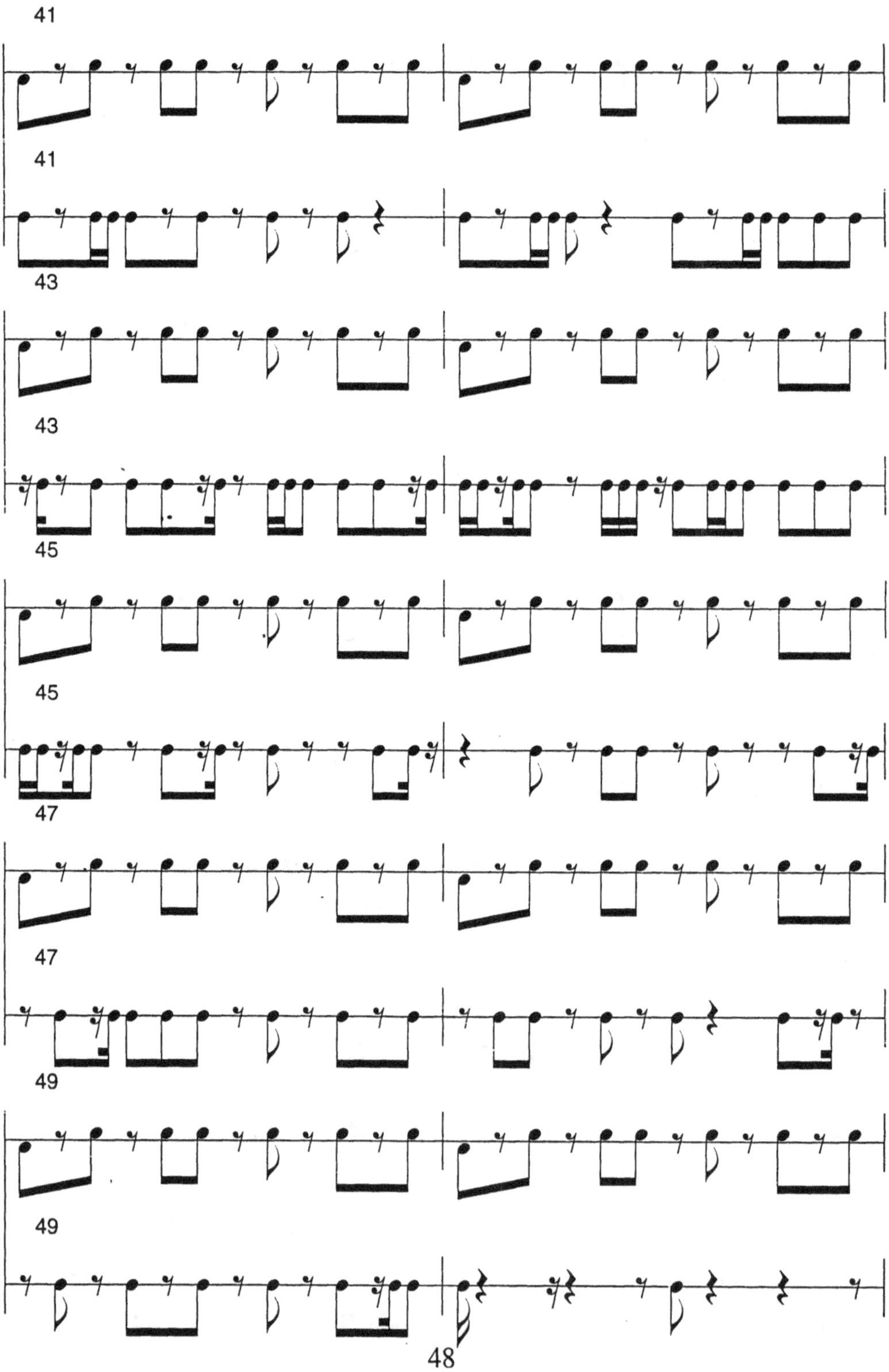

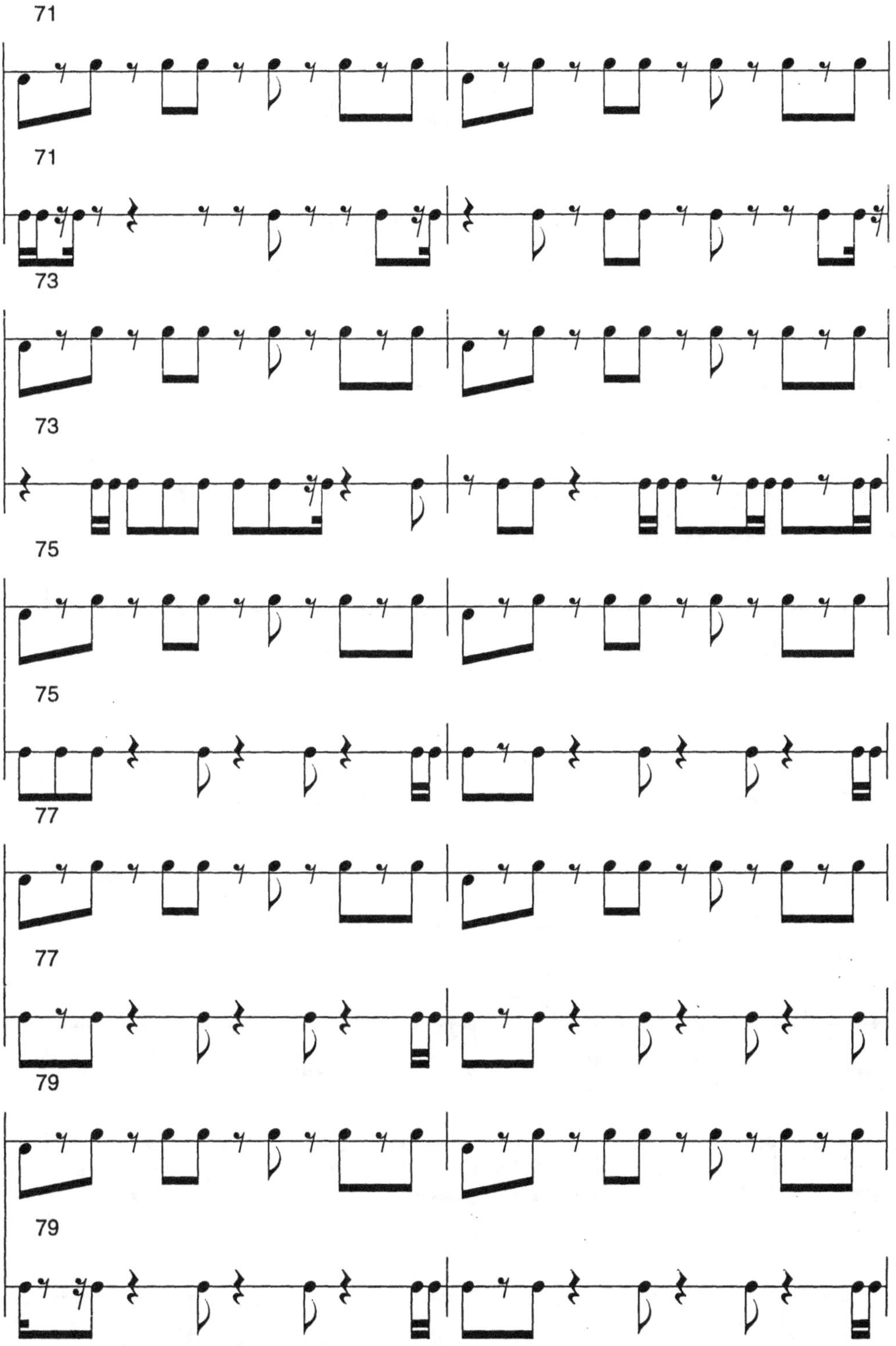
71
71
73
73
75
75
77
77
79
79

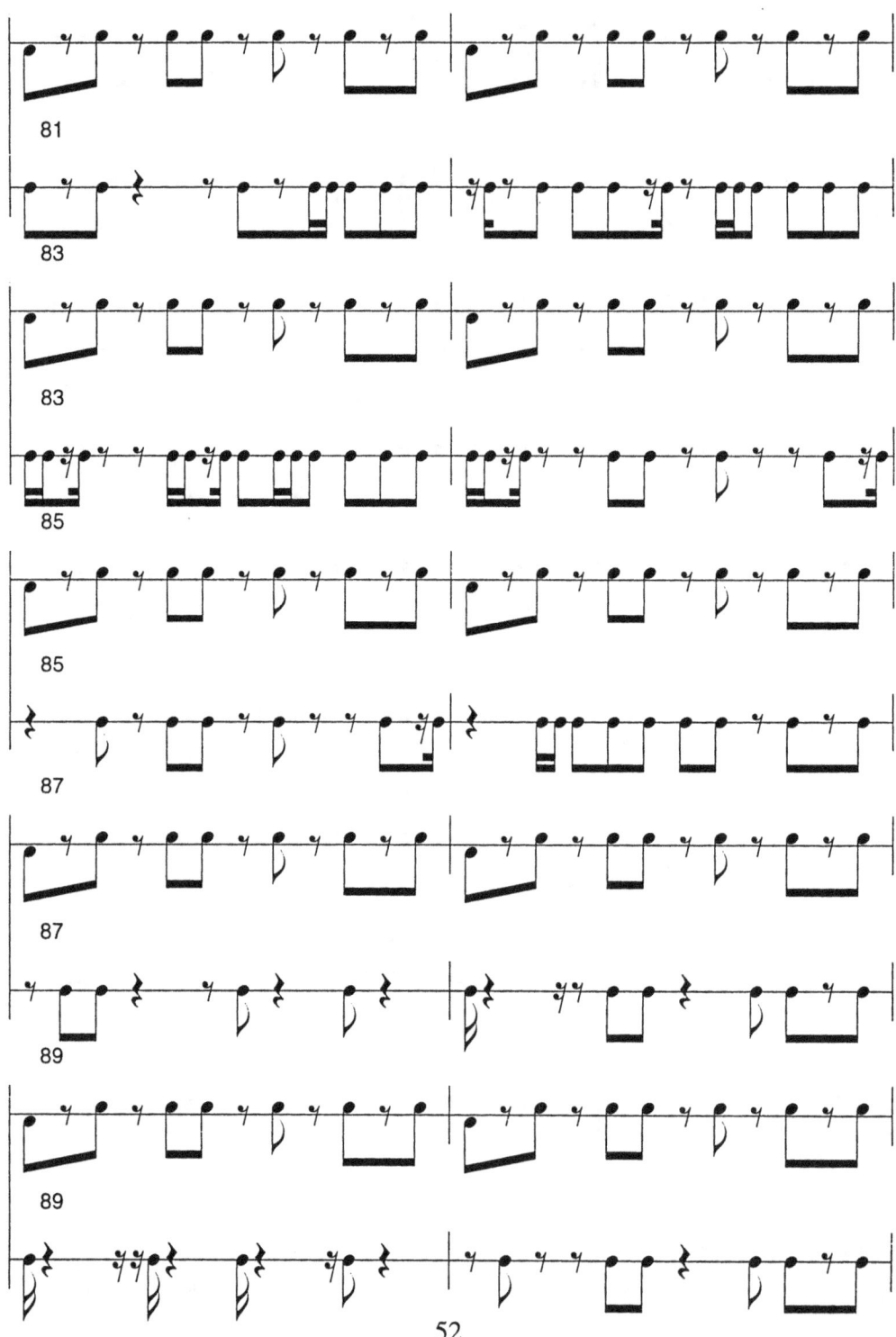

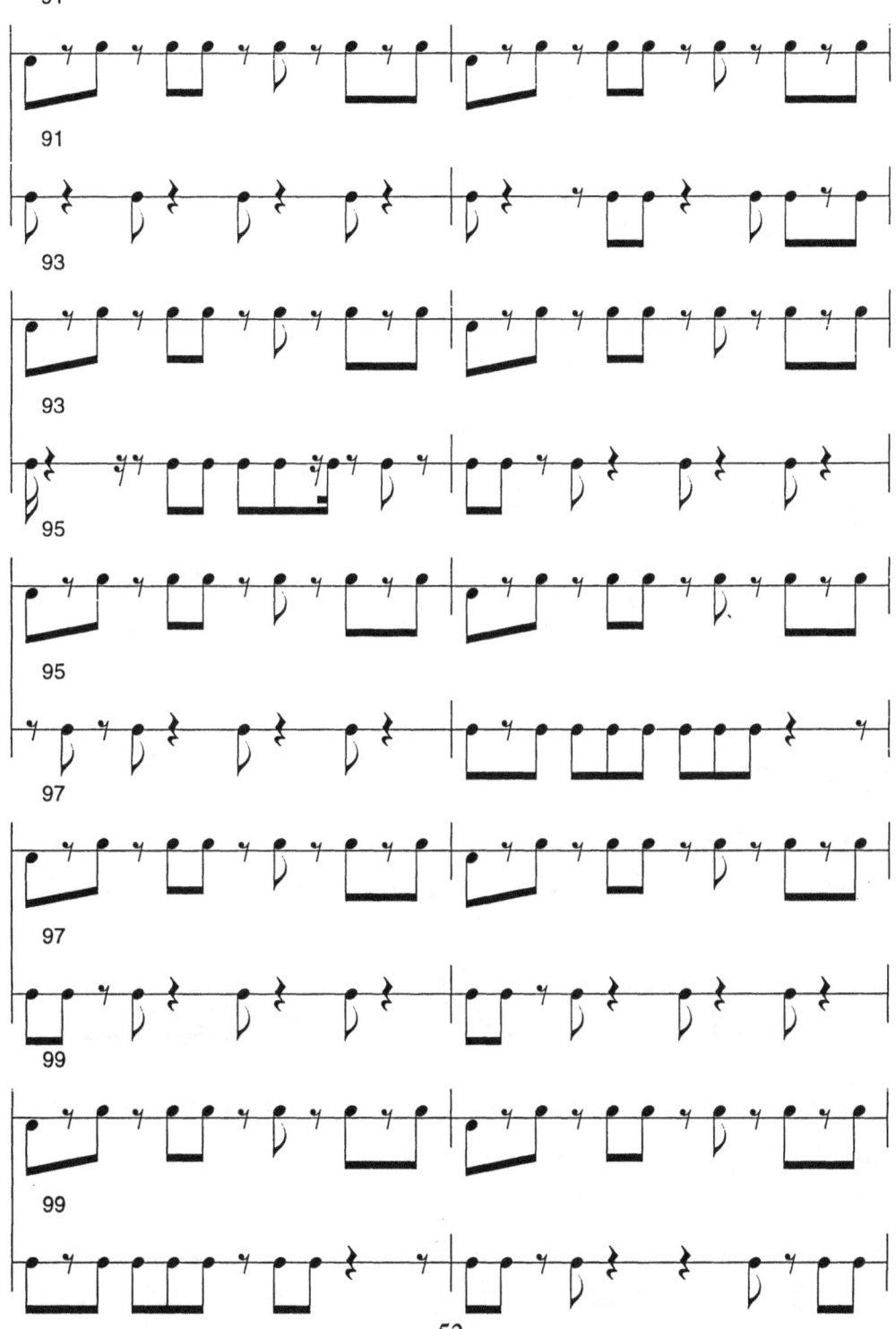

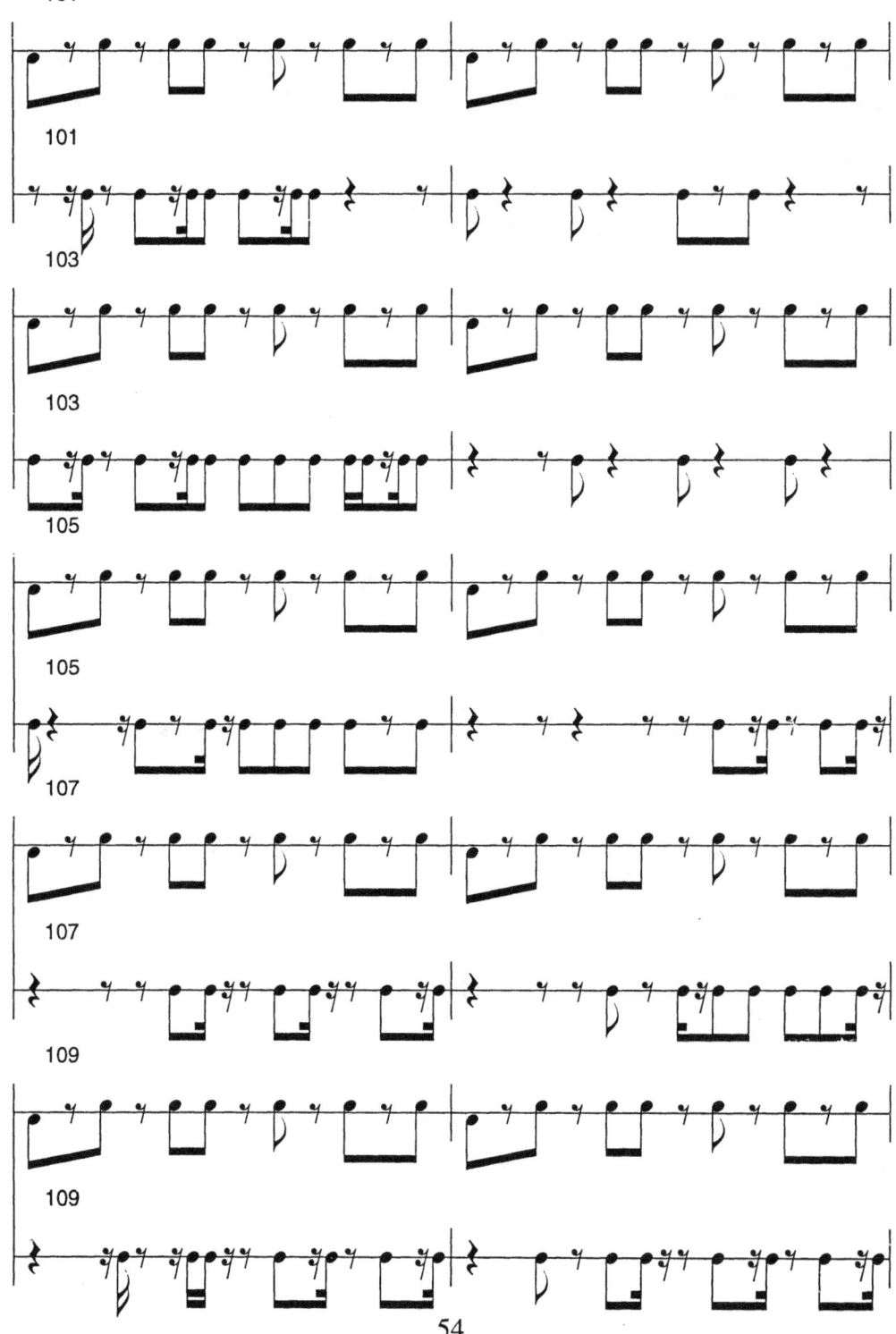

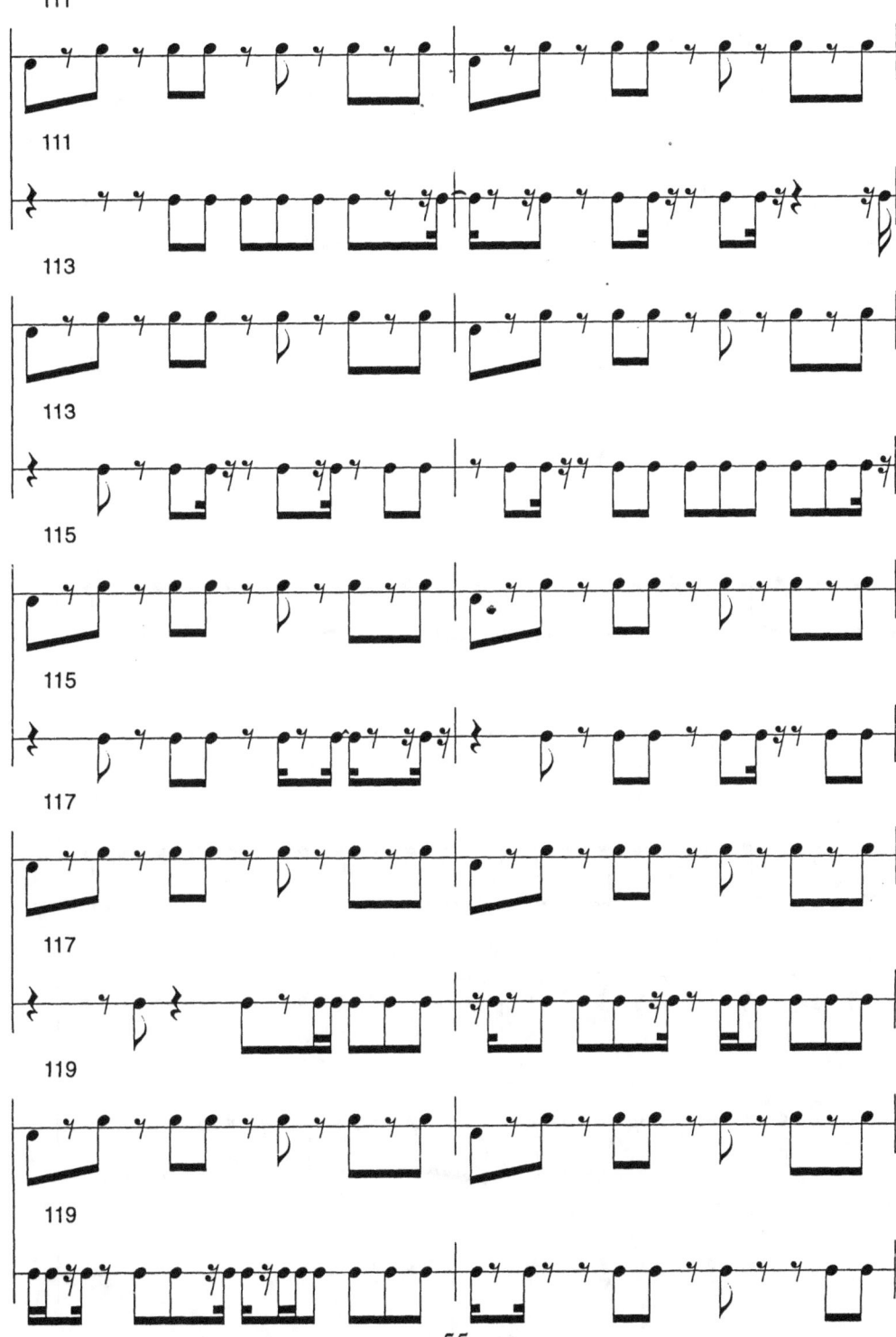

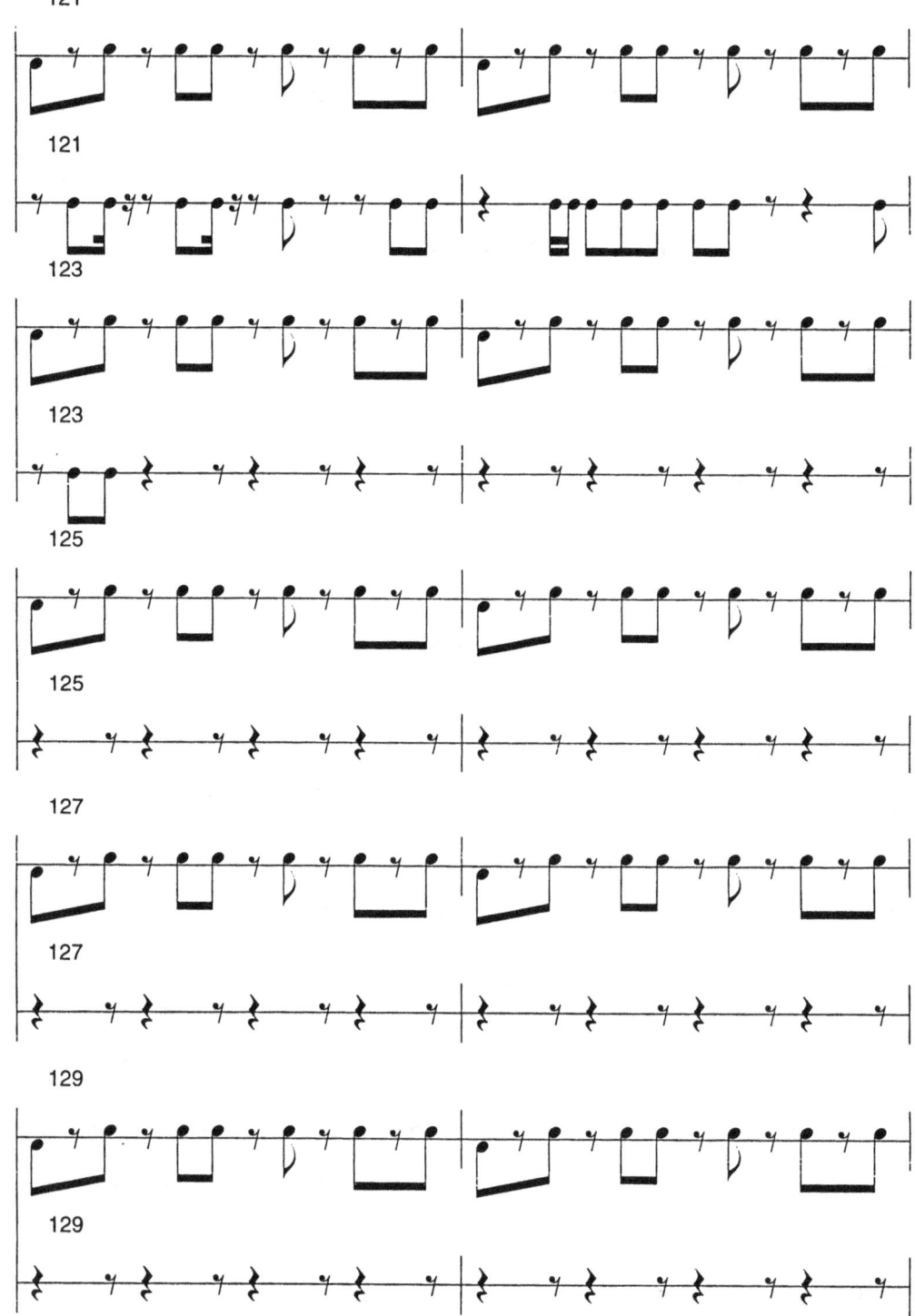

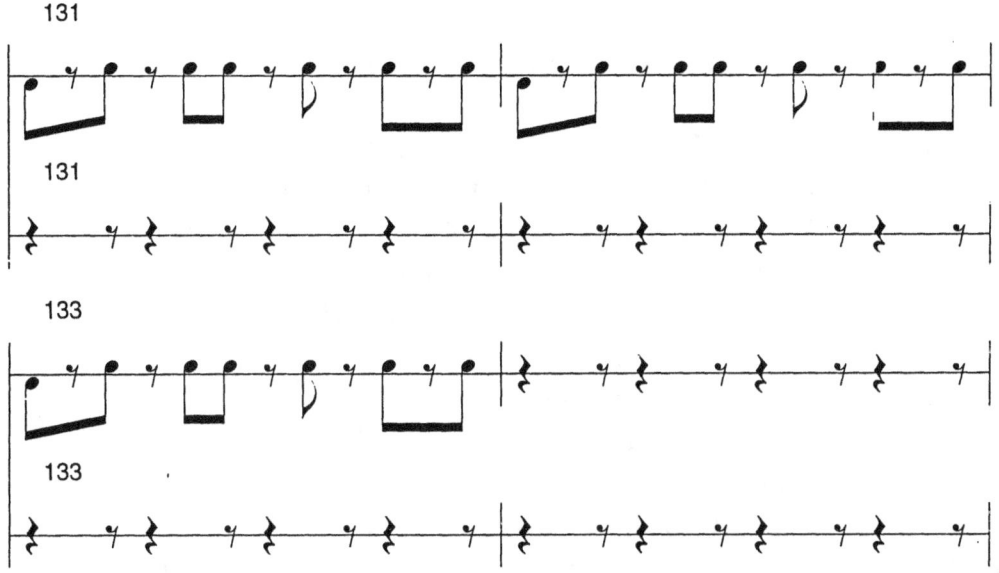

SELECT BIBLIOGRAPHY

Agawu, Kofi. *African Rhythm : A Northern Ewe Perspective.* Cambridge : Cambridge University Press, 1995.

Anku, Willie. *Structural Set Analysis of African Music 1. Adowa,* Legon : Soundstage Production, 1986.
Structural Set Analysis of African Music 2. Bawa, Legon : Soundstage Production, 1993.

Chernoff, John. *African Rhythm and African Sensibility.* Chicago : University of Chicago Press, 1977.

Jones, A. M. *Studies in African Music*, Vol. 2. London : Oxford University Press, 1959.

Locke, David. *Drum Gahu : A Systematic Method for an African Percussion Piece.* Crown Point, Indiana : White Cliffs Media Company, 1967.

Nketia, J. H. *Drumming in Akan Communities of Ghana.* Edinburgh : Thomas Nelson and Sons Ltd., 1963.

www.ingramcontent.com/pod-product-compliance
Lightning Source LLC
Chambersburg PA
CBHW081422230426
43668CB00016B/2326